The Things I Wish I'd Known

Various contributors

Edited by Michelle Gant

Cover design by Christina Leigh

For Thea

May you and all the little girls in the world know that
anything is possible for you.

Your potential is limitless.

Thank You

Thank you from the bottom of my heart to:

Lorna Blackmore, Sarah Dennis, Hayley Edwards, Steph Allen, Vicky Etheridge, Carole Paz-Uceira, Cassie Watts, Marie Connell, Gemma Sandwell, Leanne Bridges, Teika Marija Smits, Emma Scott Smith, Vicki Haverson, Lisa Dymond, Ronda Jackson, Daisy Reynolds Haley Minns, Jacqueline Fry, Suzanna Wood, Fiona Tait, and, Michelle Atkinson

Thank you for sharing your stories.

And thank you to everyone who has supported the project and this book.

Michelle Gant, February 2023

Contents

Introduction

A few years ago, I looked at my daughter and thought: there are so many things I want you to know. Things that I now know, knowledge gained through experience, through making mistakes, through learning along the way.

So, I had an idea for a book. Things I'd learnt that I wanted to pass on. An idea that never blossomed amidst the busyness of life, and so many other priorities to focus my attention on.

Only, recently that idea remerged but this time took shape as a collaborative project, and I invited other women to share the things that they've learned. The response was fantastic.

And, so here it is. **The Things I Wish I'd Known.** I am so grateful to the amazing women who have shared their inspiring, moving, uplifting, thought-provoking stories and knowledge within these pages.

Together with the personal essays, there are also tips and suggestions throughout this book which is intended to be a supportive guide. (Think of it as having a friend in book form beside you, sharing their stories and ideas).

Finally, at the end of the book, you'll find space for you to write down your thoughts, ideas, reflections, goals, hopes – whatever you wish. Because the fact is, whilst we're sharing our tales and tips, you're the only person who knows what's right for you, what you need, and what you want to – and can – achieve.

Words have power and through this book, we also want to make a difference for other women. And so, 100 per cent of all royalties will be donated to Women's Aid.

'When women support each other incredible things happen.'

Michelle Gant, February 2023

No regrets just lessons learned

Lorna Blackmore

Although everything I have experienced has made me who I am today, there are some things I know now that I think might have helped me on my journey. I could have written so much more but trying to keep it brief and digestible!

I have no regrets – certainly there are areas I think I could have done better but I have learned from those and am grateful for the interesting, colourful, wonderful life I have been gifted.

Having a child is hard work

Be prepared for the angst, the sleepless nights (for various, different reasons throughout their life!), a complete lack of knowledge of what it really takes to bring up a child in this world. That said, don't beat yourself up for not knowing what to do next – every experience is unique for every parent and child – live your experience with your child and don't strive for perfection, it doesn't exist. Just do you. The greatest thing you can do is love your child and keep on loving.

Don't compare

I have compared myself to so many people in the past and occasionally it still creeps in. But it can send you into an insecurity spin. So what if they have the smarter child, bigger car, better qualifications. So what if their life looks amazing; have a seemingly better job, look smarter, are faster on the track – whatever it is – don't compare. It will eat away at you – not them – and moves you away from achieving what you want to achieve. Invest in you, focus on you, understand your gift to the world and trust the timing of your life.

I am not in control of what people say about me

I can't stop people talking about me or control what they think or say about me. Determine what you can control. All I can do is make sure I live by my values, do good, be good and know that I have done everything to the best of my ability. If I don't feel I have, then that's on me. Not everyone will like me, so what! Keep moving forward with your development. You are in control of your behaviour, attitude, thoughts and what you say about yourself. Be kind to yourself.

Trust your gut instinct

You will know whether something is right or wrong for you, and if it feels wrong in any way, if it rubs, or makes you doubtful, get up and leave, or, depending on the circumstances, say no thank you. Speak out if it's a work thing – even if you feel you're the lone voice – if everyone wants to go left and you think it should be straight ahead, say. If everyone still goes left you've at least expressed your feelings. You have these instincts for guidance – nurture and utilise them.

Appreciate today

We only get today for one day – appreciate and learn from it. Take the pictures. As cliché as it sounds – smell the flowers. Enjoy the sunrise and sunsets, marvel at nature, breathe in the fresh air, enjoy the work, enjoy the dinner, the get-togethers, the laughter, the love. You're never going back to that moment. Relish it.

There is nothing wrong with telling someone how you feel

Sarah Dennis

It's funny when you get to the ripe old age of 51, how so many things seem so obvious and you think to yourself: 'if only I'd known that in my youth!' Of course, it doesn't matter what age we are, we are still learning, but there are some lessons that can take years to fully grasp.

I'm sure a number of us in this collection will have written about low self-esteem and self-worth, because so many of us seem to suffer from it. I often wonder how it starts. Should I be blaming my parents for not praising me enough?! Men in my life who seemed to think women should be seen and not heard? Who knows? But I do know that it can impact on so much of your life.

In my work as an image consultant, I remember one lady who came to have her colours assessed. She was recently divorced, feeling very low, and told me that several of her friends and colleagues had said she was looking old and tired! She was crushed by this and began to doubt everything about herself. My first reaction when I saw her was what beautiful skin she had. (Not because I am that shallow, but because it's my job to notice these things).

It broke my heart for her that her friends had made her feel that way. They had made her feel quite down, and of course she believed they were right. She had a list of all her 'faults' to present to me.

We all do this I'm sure – I'm very good at sucking up other people's emotions and opinions to the detriment of my own. But it takes time to learn strength and to be able to say: "I appreciate what you are saying, but...." Oh, and of course, not spend the next three weeks feeling guilty about it.

There's that word we know and love! Guilt! I used to worry about what people thought of me. I felt guilty if I told them what I thought. About anything! If a friend asked what I wanted to do on a day out, my response would be "I don't miiinnnnnd!" because what if I chose something they hated, or it was all a disaster and they blamed me?! How irritating it must have been for them to never once get a decision from me!

Of course, this comes from thinking that your wants, needs, desires and fears aren't worth as much as anyone else's. Well, at 51, I am telling you that's nonsense! There is nothing wrong with telling someone how you feel, that they have upset you, annoyed you, railroaded you into something you did not want to do. Guess what will happen when you tell them? I will tell you what will happen – absolutely nothing! The world will still be round, and you will more than likely still have your friendships. They might have a little bit of a sulk about it, but so what?

What WILL happen, however, if you continue to hide your feelings, putting everyone else's needs before your own, and always bending to others will, is that you will feel angry. You could also feel insignificant. You could be taken advantage of (perhaps not intentionally). You could end up in unhealthy relationships.

We don't need to be rude or aggressive to people – we can be polite and calm but firm. Think about what YOU want. What YOU want to do. And then if you find yourself in a situation where you aren't happy, say so! Say it with confidence, say it politely and say it with meaning. Say it like Jessica Fletcher in Murder, She Wrote! Always polite, always firm, and never rude. My heroine!

You matter. You really do. There is only one of you. There wasn't a prototype and when you've left this earth, there won't be another. Imagine that! There is just you! Unique, wonderful, amazing, funny, clever you! So why would you not want everyone to see that shine through? Don't be comparing yourself to anyone else. (Ok, I'm not a saint, I still do this at times). Don't be thinking your thoughts and feelings don't count because they ABSOLUTELY DO! You will say and do daft things in your lifetime (I seem to have said and done enough daft things for several lifetimes), but this is what life is about. A cliché, but true.

So, I guess I wish I had known its ok to say how you feel.

It's ok to disagree with other people. The world will not end if you do. It's ok to be strong and not follow the

crowd. Make daft mistakes. Laugh at yourself! And stop
worrying what others think and stop with the guilt.

Go be happy!

A thing learnt along the way

'Be kind to yourself and then
let your kindness fill the world'

Kindness is integral to our wellbeing and our happiness - and it starts with being kind to ourselves.

We can be kind to ourselves by stopping, by listening to our own needs, by taking time for the things that we want to do – not just need to do; by valuing ourselves, by demonstrably knowing that we matter. By giving ourselves recognition. By giving ourselves space – and time, especially time.

And when we do these things, not only are we role modelling kindness to those around us, but we are also better equipped to be kind to others.

Everyone is insecure sometimes

Hayley Edwards

Growing up I aways felt like an outsider. I was never really 'good' at anything. I'm not sporty, very clever, or musical (my family still haven't recovered from the 'learning to play the clarinet years') and it meant I was on the edge looking in. And I was looking in on people who were cool, popular, clever, and never insecure. Or so it seemed.

When I started in my career, I hadn't studied or been formally trained to do what I do, so naturally I thought I wasn't good enough. I based a lot of what I do on my gut instinct, whether something 'feels' like the right way to go or the solution to a problem. And again, I watched others who always knew the answer. People who weren't scared to stand up and share an opinion, talk publicly, or argue their case. Those people were never nervous, no matter what was thrown at them.

I have been building my career since 2005. During those early days I started to notice tiny cracks. Chinks in people's armour, showing the bits that generally they didn't show.

They started off as flashes, hints of insecurity. I would notice these strong, successful professionals could occasionally flush when asked a question, make a mistake in a meeting, or stumble over their words.

But surely these talented humans didn't get insecure? Turns out they did. And once I understood that I started to pay attention to the things that made me feel most insecure, and try to get plans in place to help. It started with simple practical things, so for instance when going to a meeting I would take my laptop (and charger – always the charger!) so if asked a question I could find the answer. No-one expected me to be able to answer everything off the top of my head. I had put that pressure on myself. Having the mechanism in place to say, "oh great question, let me just check," is totally fine. The insecurity of not knowing the answer was taken away in the simplest way.

Once I had got my bank of practical defence mechanisms underway, I started to think about how I could work on the emotional side. I think the key to doing that is identifying your strengths and using them to your advantage. I like to think I'm a good listener and can remember things that are important to someone else. I am also able to build relationships, and can generally find some common ground with people.

That's great Hayley, so what?

Well the 'what' is I used those skills to help lead a conversation. If you're leading it, you're less likely to be asked questions you don't know. You can also help support other people by asking how the recently adopted rescue cat is they mentioned a few weeks ago. By talking to and being interested in them, you are actually settling yourself.

By pretending to be confident, and honing my natural skills – which we all have, I promise – I can walk into a room, give the impression of confidence and allow myself time to acclimatise, regulate my breathing and settle the sweaty palms. Normally.

I was talking to a very wise friend about this recently and she described it as being a pufferfish. Make yourself look big and scary, and you don't get eaten. In my case, make yourself lead the conversation and you don't look insecure. The old adage 'fake it 'til you make it,' really is true. Shoulders back, plaster a smile on your face (if you can) breathe, and use your natural talents to hide your insecurities.

Practice has meant I find it much easier to summon up my inner pufferfish when I need her now. But I still feel nervous and rife with insecurities when I go to a networking event, challenge someone's opinion or stand up on a stage to speak. I may not look it, but one feel of my palm or glance at my flushed chest will tell you otherwise!

But I promise, if you give yourself enough time you can develop your own resilience toolkit, unique to you and your own special abilities. And you'll flourish. Take it from me, the scared kid looking in.

A career choice isn't for life

Steph Allen

I was that child who knew exactly what was going to happen in life! At the age of ten, I'd been enjoying cooking for some years and was determined to become a Home Economist, writing recipe books, delivering cookery demonstrations, and creating wonderful food to be used in adverts!

So, there it was; settled. I went through grammar school; chose 'O' levels (that dates me!) and 'A' levels that would support my quest and then, when many of my year were off to university (in the sixties fewer people went), I enrolled in a specialist college to take the National Association for Home Economics Education Diploma. I loved it and after two years I was able to gain amazing experiences working on the team designing the first fan oven, travelling the UK demonstrating cookery to groups such as Women's Institutes, and contributing to recipe books. You might think that was perfect - an achievement of a long-term goal. It was, but then for a range of reasons I left my special North London and moved to

Norfolk! Lovely place - fifty years on I have a wonderful life in beautiful Norwich, however when I moved, there were no Home Economist jobs around - in fact only three organisations it seemed, even had a Home Economics team!

New house, new life - I needed a plan B! So I took a temporary job as an Admin Assistant in, what was then Post Office Telephones. To be honest, I'm sure I was a pain to my colleagues! I resented having to give up my career plans, however I quickly found that I fitted in and was promoted! Over the next twenty years (!!) I undertook a whole range of leadership development opportunities, various qualifications and rose up the ladder five or six times. I became Regional Marketing Manager and found that, when launching new products and services, I had the skills and aptitude to help people grow. That was it then, I set up the new role of Regional Training Manager (now of course, we'd say Learning and Development) and I was flying!!!

I loved every minute of this, so as you do, at the age of forty-two, I took a voluntary redundancy package; left, what was, by then BT plc and set up my own learning and development organisation. Mad? Maybe. Hard work? Yes, although certainly not as hard as it could have been! I had a blank diary for a couple of months but soon became involved in supporting women who were thinking of setting up a business as well as delivering leadership events for the local enterprise agency. Then it all happened! Work, through recommendation and repeat business, came flooding in; I was booking clients in for over two years at a time. The recession in 2008 could have been a challenge however it became clear that I could go out and attract more clients; it worked! Since then, I've worked with amazing people and learnt so much about them and their organisations. I've spoken at conferences around the UK as well as Australia, USA and China! I'm addicted to helping people get better at what they do!

Helping people also means 'helping me'. A couple of years ago I thought it would be fun to study for a professional doctorate in 'Strategic Direction and Culture' - what a great time I had and now proudly use the post-nominal 'DPhil'!!!

So now, at the age of seventy-one, with work still booked for the next year and new work coming in weekly, I'm thriving, fulfilled and we have a great quality of life! Yes, I say 'we' because my husband is not only my biggest supporter but has become a partner in the business so that we can share some clients. We met at work nearly fifty years ago and despite people's comments such as "you work together and live together, isn't that difficult?" we've had a whale of a time and hopefully this will continue. I can still use my passion for cooking through entertaining, I've not lost that love of food!

Retirement? I don't think so! Slowing down? Maybe. Would I have had this great life if I'd stuck to my childhood dream? I truly doubt it! The lesson is four-fold:

- It's great to have a childhood ambition, but it doesn't have to define you forever!
- It's always possible to change direction!
- We make our own opportunities!
- It's never too late to start again!

What else can I do?

"What else can I do?" is a great question in two ways.

When we feel like we're stuck, when things are careering out of control and happening to us - there is always, always something we can do. What's key is understanding just what that is. And this question helps us to uncover more options.

We can also ask it to build on achievements, using our feelings of success as a springboard to do even more. "If I can do that, I wonder what else I can do?"

By asking yourself "what else can I do?" you will likely discover so much more than you might ever have thought possible.

There are so many ways to be a great mum

Michelle Gant

Leaning against the kitchen worktop, waiting for the kettle to boil, I exhaled deeply.

"I feel sorry for Thea. She doesn't have a proper mum."

The thought popped into my head unbidden, and quite unexpectedly, in that brief moment of quiet solitude. And, having made its mark, it then proceeded to ricochet around my mind, leaving behind a trail of guilt and disappointment and sadness.

Even now, seven years on, as I write in my position of fairly assured confidence in my mothering skills, it is a memory that still makes me feel a little tearful. Not because of the thought – which I now know to be utter rubbish – but for that incarnation of me. I wish I could go back, give that fragile woman a hug, and tell her it wasn't true.

But. I'm getting ahead of myself.

I'm a planner by nature. I like to be organised, and control the stuff that I can control. So before we'd even decided to have our child we'd talked about how we would bring her up. Childcare, we knew, would be key and we'd been wrestling with the logistics. "I'll do it," my husband Bobby had said, simply. "I'll give up work and look after the baby." It was like a light had been switched on. That made sense, we both agreed. And, as we were on holiday, we ordered another round of drinks from the bar to celebrate our ingenuity.

But it got better. It was as if the universe was in absolute agreement with us. Because then, would you believe it, the government only went and announced shared parental leave. Which meant that we could share my maternity leave and pay. Win, win.

Our good fortune kept on coming in the shape of a straightforward pregnancy, before a little later than expected (you can't plan for that, I discovered to my frustration) we welcomed our beautiful daughter Thea. I remember my dad describing her as 'exquisite' and I can think of no better description for her. She really was.

Absolutely exquisite.

We started to get to know her. And with every passing day, we loved her more and more. But whilst my adoration scaled new heights, my confidence fell through the floor. I questioned every parental move I made. I remember once taking baby Thea out for a walk in her pram with my mum and dad and inside my anxieties were screaming. *"Is the movement of the wheels hurting her head? Is she in the right position? Is she breathing"*, I fretted as I waved my hand gently in front of her mouth (side note: I still do this now. But now the response I usually receive is "geroff Mum.")

Before too long, it was time for the switch – Bobby at home, me at work. My heart ached at the thought of being separated from my darling baby; well, to be honest it still twinges now when I am away from her for any length of time. It would though. She carries my heart. It was agonising. And yet, there was something else I felt. Excitement about getting back to work, being with other grown-ups, doing my job. And happiness too, for Bobby; after all, it was his turn now to have that special experience.

However, whenever people asked me: "Why are you going back to work?" I would always bluster and mutter and say something like "Blah blah blah financial reasons blah blah," rather than just giving the real answer which was: "Because this is what we want."

The truth was, and despite the certainty in my head when it was just the three of us, I started to doubt myself. And I felt that I was being judged as a bad mum – though for the most part, the only judging that was going on was inside my head. (However, I can still remember the one woman – a stranger – who was appalled by the path we had taken. Now, seven years on, I've got a response for her. But that ship hasn't just sailed, it's in port and disembarked).

Were we doing the right thing? Should I be the one at home? Do people think I don't love Thea enough?

Everywhere I seemed to look, other mums were doing it differently. *Better.*

These doubts and concerns danced around in my head for a long time. The fear that I wasn't doing it right as a mum could sometimes be overwhelming. Such as on the day it brought me to that ground-shaking thought standing in my kitchen:

"I feel sorry for Thea. She doesn't have a proper mum."

In my heart, I knew this thought wasn't true and as soon as it cropped up, I worked to present to myself all the reasons why I was a proper mum. And yet, I still couldn't quite shake the feeling that I wasn't up to muster.

But two things happened during that period. Or rather, two wonderful women made comments that were transformative for me.

Friend one: "You're doing an amazing job."

Friend two: "You don't have to be the best mum in the world. But you're the best mum in the world to Thea."

The fact that I can still clearly recall and distinctly remember these remarks shows how significant and important they were to me. I needed that positive reinforcement.

All mums do.

Because here's the thing. We live in a society where women are routinely pitted against each other and never is that truer than when it comes to motherhood. You're a working mum or a stay-at-home mum. You're a breastfeeding mum or a bottle-feeding mum. You're a natural nappies mum or disposable nappies mum. You're a cry it out mum or you're a mum who responds to every sob.

And let's not even go there on the unwelcome opinions routinely shared on just how many children mothers should have. Never mind the so called perfect 2.4, if you're a mother, only you know what your magic number is – 1 or 21: it ain't anybody's business but yours. It's a battleground. And it's exhausting. Especially for new mothers who may be emotionally vulnerable.

As women, we can support each other, lift each other up, and be there for one another. And I've been so lucky to have those two friends and so many other brilliant women to lend a listening ear and a kind word since I began this motherhood journey.

After all, we're sisters not rivals.

As my friends told me, and if you're a mum reading this: **You're doing an amazing job. You're the best mum that your child could ask for.**

Because what I've learnt over the last few years is that there are so very many ways to be a great mum, it's about finding the right way for you and your family.

That's the only way that matters.

Comparison is the thief of joy

We are sisters, not rivals.

And yet so often women are pitted against each other. Or sometimes, we're the ones doing the pitting.

She's prettier than me, she's got nicer clothes, a better house, a newer car, better behaved children, a more interesting life…

And of course, social media makes it even easier for us to fall into that comparison trap. Any time you pop on to Instagram you will definitely find someone who is having a better time than you. Guaranteed.

But it doesn't matter. What matters is us, our lives, our goals, our dreams. We're not comparing like for like.

One thing that can help you when you feel yourself being sucked into that comparison trap is bringing it back to all the good stuff in your life (and there's an abundance). Focus on and celebrate the things that you appreciate in your world.

And, if you see something in someone's life that you want, then use it to inspire you not deflate you.

Because it's true – comparing ourselves to others really does take away our joy.

There's no need to rush, take your time

Vicky Etheridge

Time, it's a strange concept when you think about it, and of course one of our own making. I was wondering when I really started to be aware of time, and I don't mean when I first learnt to tell the time. I remember that very clearly, along with the tantrums of frustration: "what do you mean it's almost five past three?" I screeched at my Mum as a frustrated and precise four-year-old! At what point in our lives does the construct of time become part of our daily consciousness, to the point of often becoming a dull ache of pressure that too often influences our decision making and actions?

I think I was in my teens when I first felt the weight of time and had a big decision to make. It was one of those key transition points in life, the move from A-Levels to Higher Education and the question of what to do next, and where to go to do it. I didn't even contemplate taking a gap year to buy some time, pause and explore other opportunities, I didn't think I had time. As it happened at that point I had a strong sense of self, I knew roughly what I wanted to learn, had a good idea of what I didn't want to do, and I certainly knew where I didn't want to live. Crucially, for me at least, I was given the space to make my decision and I set off on that adventure, nervous about a new beginning, but secure in my decision.

Four years later was quite a different story. I didn't handle the university to work transition with such surety, and I felt the heaviness of time and the fear of debt. I threw myself into applying for jobs through 'the milk round'. Interview after interview, selection centre after selection centre, travelling around the country. It was exhausting, nerve wracking and demoralising - I wasn't offered a single job, although came very close to several. It took me a while after that experience to appreciate that the biggest barrier to being offered one of those graduate jobs was the fact that I didn't really want any of them, and that must have been very apparent to the recruiters. What I really wanted was some certainty about what came next. In the end, I did secure a job before I'd graduated, and it was 100% the right one for me. Looking back, if only I'd known that there's no need to rush, that exploring different options and making mistakes is all part of the process of finding your way and getting to know who you are. I would have saved myself some of the stress, and feelings of rejection, of not being good enough.

As I sit here thinking and writing, I realise just how often I have felt the need to do something, to act straight away, to have certainty. I have rarely taken what I would have perceived was a risk, that is to wait and see what might come my way. Not all of these moments are big, life changing events, although some do relate to career decisions, (I have been a serial job changer until relatively recently) feeling a need to find a new challenge, to change before I got bored, to grab the next promotion. Looking back, I never waited for circumstances to change, or explored how I might be able to grow in an existing post. I looked outwards to see what might be around and grabbed it. Seizing the moment is definitely not a bad thing, but if I was advising my younger self, I think I would encourage her to explore the option of 'sticking', taking some time to 'be' before, or at least weighing it up alongside those new opportunities that might carry me off onto a different path. Because, there's no need to rush, taking your time can be enriching.

Other moments that come to mind are more day-to-day occurrences. Like the work projects devised and delivered when under pressure to make an impact and do something big. Only to reflect after the (stressful) event, that if I'd taken my time and not rushed into delivery, the event or piece of work might have been more impactful, and less stressful. Or, when my boys were very young, rushing around to give them experiences, to go to places, to do things, to make new friends. Yet now, my memories aren't of those places we went to, and the playdates we shared but of the slower times at home, reading stories snuggled on the sofa, making presents for Daddy and random Lego models. So, I'd say "slow down, take your time, there's no need to rush. Memories and moments of joy appear in the mundane and the everyday, not just on the grand days out and big occasions."

Age and hindsight, what a marvellous pairing, almost up there with cheese and crackers (which I think is something I enjoy more with age by the way!). Ironically, as I get older and the time I have left diminishes, I favour slowing down, making time to think and reflect, to watch and listen to those around me. As my boys grow older and approach important milestones, I hear myself encouraging them to take their time, to give things a try, to be open to possibilities and opportunities, because you can never be sure what lies ahead, what might change and shift around you. And so, I find myself looking back and wondering how things might have been different if I'd only known to take my time, there's no need to rush.

Friendships evolve and grow over time

Carole Paz-Uceira

I am middle aged. I have a husband, two kids, a dog, a cat, a full-time job, and a mortgage. Days, weeks, and months pass by in an instant, crowded with work, kids' activities, and general mundanity. My husband often works away, leading to a carefully choreographed juggling act ensuring that the essentials are in place.

Don't get me wrong, I am happy with my lot and eternally grateful for what I have. Our household is full of love. My husband and I were good mates before we got together and we are quite happy on the sofa watching TV, listening to music, and tucking into snacks and the odd glass of wine or two (OK, bottle). My two boys are full of life and endless energy. They amaze me every day with their developing personalities, constant questioning, and zest for learning about everything.

Sometimes, however, I need to escape the noise, the routines, and the responsibility. It is easy to forget sometimes who I am. An hour or two helps me to restore some sanity. Often this is via a dog walk listening to a podcast or yoga class. True escapism though is meeting up with my friends, in particular those long-term friends who I have known since before responsibilities took hold. Before I was a wife and a mother.

Most of my closest friends have been part of my life for decades. Thinking back to my twenty-somethings, life was uncomplicated. We said yes to everything. I did my share of travelling, building memories of far-flung places and having adventures. These include escaping a police raid on the back of a motorbike in Vietnam and falling for a Scottish bloke wearing a Playboy shirt whilst backpacking down the west coast of Mexico. Surprisingly enough that relationship didn't last! My friend and I were contestants on the little-known TV show called Come Fly With Me and ended up in Barbados, being eliminated from the show after coming last on a beach assault course. I loved the outdoors with a passion. Whenever we had a spare weekend we would end up camping in the Lake District. This was camping without luxuries, often in a basic site in Langdale that was little more than a farmer's field. I remember one night partying in a local pub and then walking back to our tent naked – getting a shock when the farmer shone his light into our tent in the middle of the night. We loved hiking up the mountains, and eventually this led to me developing a love for rock climbing. We were all footloose and fancy free.

For a while, when my boys were young, I just did not have the capacity to invest enough time in my friendships. Thank God my long-time friends stuck by me and were willing to accept that I was incommunicado at times and that I could no longer be spontaneous or say yes to everything. Now that my life has entered a new phase, past the baby years when I was needed 24-7, I am really enjoying the changing nature of my friendships. When the hubby is away I will get them round for a deep dive interrogation about all that has occurred over recent weeks. We expel all frustrations and worries. It feels like a therapy session and I'm always rejuvenated. We support each other through the many ups and downs of life. We just 'get' each other and importantly no effort is required or explanations needed. Staying in is just as good as going out.

On a recent trip to the Lakes with a group of mates we stayed in a luxury cottage rather than a farmer's field. We didn't walk up to the top of the highest fells, but found a gorgeous circular low level route and ended up 'dirty dining' – going straight to the pub covered in mud. We then all admitted we wanted to go back to the cottage early in time for Strictly. I felt so much love for the women around me, in our pajamas, all lamenting that Giovanni Pernice had already been booted off, whilst talking about our collective journeys towards perimenopause and how we can be more environmentally savvy.

I know that I get my love of friendships from my mam. She is in her mid-seventies (sorry, Mam) and still has a fabulous set of friends that she relies on for her own escapism. She meets them on a Monday for walking club, on Tuesday at church, on Fridays for coffee in a local pub (always in the same corner booth) and at the two Women's Institute groups that she attends. She is also part of a WI splinter group called 'The Bad Taste Girls' who enjoy regular meals out and endless gossiping. I can see how much they all mean to each other, and how they have been there for each other over the years through good times and bad.

As I get older I can reflect on how my friendships have evolved. Whilst our partners and family circumstances may have changed, the friendships remain and have developed over the years to an even deeper connection. I now know the true value of those friendships, and the importance that they have on maintaining my mental wellbeing and overall levels of happiness. I would be lost without them.

I know that when I reach retirement I will still be escaping with my ladies. I know that there will be new adventures, perhaps with a little less drama and more cups of herbal tea. Or maybe it will go full circle and I will grow old disgracefully. Cherish and nurture your friendships.

A thing learnt along the way

You are not alone

Whatever it is that you need, there is help out there. To support you to achieve your goals, to find solutions, to come up with ideas, or to help you if you are struggling.

Friends, family, colleagues, mentors, professionals – there is always someone who can lend a helping hand.

And, as women we can always reach out and support each other.

Life is for adventuring, not observing

Cassie Watts

I walked out of the bus station in Cancun in Mexico with my four children in tow and eight suitcases all held close. My husband had gone to sort something out, my phone battery was dying, the kids were asking for food and our coach to Chiquilla was shortly departing. With my stress levels rising, I stopped on the road to slow my breath and get in the moment. I thought to myself - this is real, we are really here and this is all part of the experience. I grabbed the kids some food, made our way back into the station and hoped my husband would be there. Of course, he joined us a few minutes later. It was lucky I had got the kids some food and had to get cash out because they needed the bathroom right before our two hour coach journey and it was 20 pesos each. We boarded the coach on time with minutes to spare.

I had a lot of these moments around that time. Waves of pride and awe and then hints of disbelief and guilt. We had sold our home, most of our possessions, my husband quit his job and I had paused my business to take our children on an adventure that would last for eight months. Had we made the right decision? Should we have just bought another home right away? Sometimes I still question that but as I hear the children discuss our adventure and the things they miss from it, I feel periodic security that we made the right decision for our family. All I knew was that we had an opportunity and I would absolutely regret it if we didn't take it.

I remember falling asleep one night on a farm deep in the Costa Rican wild; the pigs slept underneath our cabin and there was a family of bats right on the other side of the mosquito net that was inches from my face. I had my trusty neck pillow and ear plugs to drown out the noise of the cockerel that seemingly never slept and I breathed steadily in time with the floor fan that hummed all night long. That night I woke up so many times, unable to fall into a deep sleep, mostly content with just listening and breathing but my mind intermittently whirred with 'what ifs'. The kitchen on the farm was outside, mouse droppings and bugs were plentiful, and we got sick from the lukewarm tap water so we had some serious adjusting to do. As the days went by, with the help of two friends, I learnt to observe and sit more, to experience the moments without wants and expectations. They invited me to be more patient with myself and allow some space for acclimatisation. The farm surroundings were so bright and beautiful, rich in colour, flora, and life! The animals kept the children busy, and I even began to enjoy washing our clothes with the manual washing machine! There was something in it, something simple and satisfying.

I don't remember the exact moment I realised that what I'd hoped would happen was happening but I remember thinking "Yes! It's happening!!!" I was slowing down. I was noticing more. Being more present. Breathing it all in. Allowing myself to enjoy and experience all that there was. I investigated new sounds as my intrigue grew with this new world we were in. In fact, one time I heard a rustling in the leaves and soon found it was an iguana about three feet long. We had chicks on the farm so we were on the lookout for iguanas as they snacked on our little furry friends! As I got closer it scuttled up the nearest tree, I moved around to get a better view but it too moved around the trunk to keep out of view. This continued for a few rounds, we had a little game of hide and seek going!

We moved on to a town called Jaco. I stopped a homeless man and using Google translate I asked him if he was hungry. He said: "I can't read your screen." He was a 68-year-old Canadian man that had been in Costa Rica for over ten years. I sat myself down next to him and we spoke for the next little while. I spent a few afternoons with John, leant against a shop window learning about his life and what had brought us both here to this moment. We shared a cooked chicken and stories from our lives. He was reading a Jack Reacher book - one he had found some months before but that was the only English book he had. Leaving Jaco, we moved on to Uvita. There we found a mother and daughter from the USA who ran an English book library. In it we found a Jack Reacher book and a week later we took a detour back through Jaco to take it to John. I couldn't find him. He was always in the same few spots but I couldn't find him. I asked local shop assistants and they said he hadn't been there all week. I wrote a note in the book and passed it onto them to give to John if he should come back. I'll never know if he ever got it or how he is now. I often think about John and the openness we shared. There were no barriers, no judgements, and no 'should be'. His connection was a gift to me at that time.

I look back at the adventuring we did with great fondness. We each have a deep nostalgia that aches in our hearts for that wonderful time. I am so proud of the courage and patience that we met the tricky situations with. Also the stillness and gratitude we embraced the wonderful times with. I am their mother and his wife but mostly I am me. I am a woman who feels a great desire to protect childhood, to pursue all that is adventurous and brave. I am determined to live an intentional, fun, and full life.

I learnt many things about myself and the world we live in over those eight months and I'd like to share one of them here; 'life Is for adventuring, not observing'. So that's yes to experiencing, yes to receiving, yes to forgiveness, courage and newfound joys and a huge, big yes to me. In saying yes to myself, I learnt that it's ok for other people (even though they care so much about me) to not understand or see my path clearly because as long as I do, I'm going to be ok. Not just ok but really, really fantastic! I even began to enjoy the experience of being brave when it felt scary. I stepped into myself in a new way that I didn't know was possible. My light grew brighter, my experiences felt more poignant and everyday joys were held closer. In gaining victory of the self there comes a sweetness of achievement and a savouring of all that comes with it.

I did that. But most importantly, I'm doing that. An ever-evolving beautiful process of self-discovery and liberating exploration.

Life begins at the end of your comfort zone

Our comfort zone is nice. It's cosy here. Reassuring, safe, and sometimes we need to stay here.

But, there is a whole different world waiting to be discovered at the end of our comfort zone. In this place we can grow, develop, and find new things.

And we don't have to take giant leaps into the unknown; it could be something as simple and small as swapping your usual toppings for something new when you're dialing in your pizza takeaway order.

What's more, stepping outside your comfort zone will likely drive your appetite for innovation and new experiences – and who knows where that could lead?

I've found my place in this world

Marie Connell

It's hard enough for us all to find our place in this world - somewhere we feel comfortable and content. Growing up as a teenager I remember having the feeling that I would never find mine. I was born with a disability - I have a congenital limb deficiency - or no lower left arm - and grew up very shy, lacking in confidence, and always feeling uncomfortable with how I looked.

I enjoyed primary school but at secondary school, I was bullied. Many kids who are 'different' have experienced this at school - some say it makes them stronger and more able to cope with whatever life throws at them - but it's still an unpleasant and difficult time - and you think it's never going to stop. For me it was not too bad - just some occasional name calling, pushing, and shoving and one particular girl who wanted to fight me on the school bus all the time! Despite my disability I was good at sport - very good - I captained all the teams in hockey, netball, tennis, basketball, and rounders. I loved gymnastics and swimming - so of course, the bullying reduced as bullies sense weakness - and I was able to show strength by being better than the bullies at sport. Being on the sporting pitch or court during PE lessons, lunchtime training and after school matches was a very happy place for me. However away from it I felt self-conscious and was convinced that all people saw when they looked at me was a young girl who looked slightly odd.

But the bullying did have a long-term impact on me - in that I hated any kind of confrontation. So, as I approached adulthood, I would walk away from any confrontation instead of standing up for myself. I had a very fractured relationship with my mother from a very early age. I realise now that she probably had some mental health issues but I was unhappy, and I left home at 17 as I could not deal with the continual confrontation and anger that she directed at me. I was homeless for a while until a string of weird coincidences led me to being able to find my own place and able to start to build my own life.

After managing to find a job at 16 - university was not an option for me then - I then started to fumble my way through life - but I still cared deeply about what people thought of me and I felt that everyone was staring, pointing, and laughing about the fact that I looked different to most other people. I could not find a way to get around this - so most of the time I hid my disability if I could. Which is fine during the winter - but during warmer weather I detested wearing t shirts and vest tops. The only time it did not bother me was when I was competing for a local athletics club whether it be training or weekend meeting fixtures. During these times, which I loved, the insecurities and negative thoughts just disappeared.

After a few more years in a few different jobs, a failed short marriage as well as three years living abroad, I moved to work in London as I found a job working for the police. I thrived in this environment. No one there cared that I had one hand. As long as I was able to do my job - they embraced my skills, my ability, my desire to give 100% all the time and my confidence levels started to soar. They sent me on professional and personal promotions in a short space of time. Then they asked me to think about delivering some training around disability awareness and diversity issues. Before I knew it, I had a senior management position with a team of over 40 members of staff and I was talking to police officers about diversity and disability. My insecurities and lack of confidence did not completely disappear but certainly reduced and I also found the strength to deal with any confrontation which, working in a police environment, did occasionally come my way. I had found the same sense of achievement that I felt when playing sport and doing athletics as a child and young adult, during my working life - and I finally felt, in my thirties, that I was dealing with my demons.

I worked for the police for 15 years until commuting in and out of London became too difficult and I moved back to Norfolk, wanting something more local. I remember feeling that I had the skills, confidence, and ability to take on something in a different sector and I ended up being the chief executive of a local charity - a job that involved networking and meeting new people all the time. Not once did I worry about what those people thought about me and the fact that I have a disability. I was content, happy, and self-confident.

My relationship with my mother continued to be very difficult and the anxiety and stress levels involved in trying to maintain some kind of contact with her made everyday life difficult. So finally, in my forties I had enough strength to stand up to her and permanently cut my ties with her. I knew at this moment that I had truly found my place in this world. I had the mental toughness, the confidence, and the ability to make the hardest decision I had ever made to stop the continual confrontation and be able to come to terms with it. I still find some days such as Mother's Day quite difficult to deal with - and have the very occasional feelings of envy towards some of my friends who have a loving mother/daughter relationship - but these negative feelings do not last long, and I am able to manage these feelings in a more positive way.

Now, in my mid-fifties, I am on a very even keel. I am happy with the choices I have made that have led me to where I am now. I will always be grateful to the Police for giving me the environment I needed to thrive and feel valued. It was also the place I met my husband and we have been together for almost 25 years. Negative thoughts about my disability simply do not exist - my insecurities now are around my wrinkles, my greying hair and my aching joints! I have the know-how and life skills to avoid confrontation if I need to but also the confidence and strength to not be afraid to challenge it. I have found my place in this world.

I am a Highly Sensitive Person – who can help others

Gemma Sandwell

I remember being sat on the train, tears rolling down my face, weird looks from other commuters as the countryside flashed by outside as I bid farewell to London. I remember the tense neck and head and chest pain that cut like a knife…

This was a weekly occurrence for me, in my corporate job in Financial Services, I worked in London frequently. Not one workday went by that didn't end in me uncontrollably crying on the way home, not one weekend followed without cancelled plans with friends, illness, and an inability to leave the house.

I had countless therapies and thousands of pounds spent to try and resolve this, it made no sense to me, I wanted to be the 'career woman'. I was driven to succeed, and these feelings were blocking me from what I thought was my dream life. I spent a lot of time frustrated when I couldn't heal these problems and through frustration I numbed myself with alcohol on weekends. Many weekends I decided to push through, see friends and socialise even when my body was screaming at me to stop.

This was my life for many years.

This was all before I knew I was a Highly Sensitive Person (HSP).

I was driving one day and listening to a podcast and the podcaster was talking about her sensitivities, the more I listened the more I realised she was resonating with me. For the first time ever I felt like someone understood what I was going through. She shared about these feelings being HSP, "what was this HSP thing I pondered?" this sounds like me?! So, onto Google I went and I found the research and book by Dr Elaine Aron 'The Highly Sensitive Person'.

Basically 15-20% of us are born with more sensory processing receptors in our brain, so we get overwhelmed easier by lots of sensory input. We feel very deeply because of this and we process things much more deeply (and are prone to overthinking because of the ways our brains work!).

Everything suddenly slotted into place and I understood why I was drawn to study Psychology in the earlier years of my adult life and went onto specialising in Positive Psychology (which was ironically what I was trying to teach in Financial Services in London when I used to cry on the train!) I'd stumbled into Positive Psychology (along with energy clearing in the later days) and I knew that my life did feel different when I tapped into those tools that I taught others, this now made sense to me knowing the science.

As HSPs those extra sensory processing receptors are much more likely to trigger the fight/flight response as we get overwhelmed easier. Positive Psychology acts as a really sustainable 'hack' to bring the fight/flight response down as it fuels the logical and creative parts of our brain.

In 2019 I was invited to speak at TEDx Norwich about Mindfulness (another life saving tool!) and Positive Psychology. I didn't fully know how to balance my life as a

HSP at that stage but I was starting to listen to my body and I now know I was intuitively doing what the science showed (not just the neuroscience but the Quantum Physics I later went onto research too!)

I had seven minutes to stand on stage and deliver my talk which I had to remember word for word and I had a huge timer clock in front of me (no pressure!)

All the other obligations and worries fell away as I knew I wanted to achieve my lifelong dream to be on that stage. Just five years previous I had such extreme anxiety I couldn't speak to five people let alone the 23,000 that were in the room and watching live that day!

I cancelled all other plans around TEDx and stayed at home to rest, recharge and practice in the two weeks leading up to it. I was part time in Financial Services at this point and running my Mindfulness business on the side. All other worries went out the window as I told my boss under all circumstances I would be working from home for the foreseeable. I didn't get the sack, in fact I got a bonus as my work improved in that time as I was listening to myself and setting boundaries (so my sensitivities calmed down!) And that day as I stood on the stage I was recharged; I'd meditated in the car in the car park, gone and got some nourishing food and prioritised sleep and rest in the weeks leading up to it.

As the seven minutes ended and I came off stage the uncontrollable sobs came back as the sound guys removed my mic and looked at me like they didn't know what the hell was going on. I had reached something incredible, I had truly taken care of myself enough to be able to live my dream of being up on that stage and get my message out to everyone. As I headed home for pizza on the sofa, instead of the networking meal planned afterwards (another thing I did to honour my needs) I felt accomplished and tired and I knew I wanted to help others through this journey too.

At the end of 2019 I left my Financial Services job fully and in 2020 I aligned my business to helping other HSPs. At that point in time I was a qualified coach and Mindfulness teacher but now I knew I needed to help others on that deeper level, I needed to raise awareness about HSP and get the word out there so that I could help to shortcut the process and reduce the pain for others from what I went through.

This has all been my big why and the reason for starting my business so I could help others to flourish and to not have to go through what I went through. In the last few years I've not only worked with clients who are HSP but clients who have HSP children and I know that I needed to speak up and share the tools that have helped me, even if I can help one parent or one child then I know the pain I went through was worthwhile.

So I wish I'd have known I was HSP and I wish I'd have known that I could speak on stage, I could run a business and help other HSPs too.

I wish I'd known that the tools I was drawn to are the tools I'd use to find balance for myself and my clients. I now live by the sea with my soulmate and our animals, I work in a cosy home office and walk to the sea and forest every day and I wish I could go back to the old version of myself and tell myself that I'd be living this life and all would be okay.

And finally I wish I'd told myself my sensitivities were superpowers and that I didn't need to change myself in anyway I just needed to listen.

*If you'd like to know more about HSP you can take the HSP test here https://hsperson.com/test/highly-sensitive-test/

A thing learnt along the way

What's the most important thing to do right now?

Our lives are full. It can sometimes feel overwhelming and hard to know where to start.

Finding focus amidst the busyness is key. And asking ourselves: what is the most important thing to do right now can be a really helpful place to start. And to come back to.

And here's a big hint: that most important thing may not be work or a chore. It could be going for a run to clear your head. Stopping to take a break. Or having a chat with a friend.

After all, we're human beings not human doings and if we want to support the 'doing', we've got to take care of the being.

Life doesn't always work out as you thought...but can end up being better than you ever imagined

Leanne Bridges

I'm sharply awoken. I turn my head to glance at the clock and it's 1am. What is that noise?

It's a child crying. It's my youngest Kate but why is she crying in the middle of the night? Maybe she's sick I think to myself, as I haul myself out of bed. It's freezing cold and the rest of the house is deadly quiet. I shiver as I stumble off to sort her out, hoping she doesn't wake the whole house.

We're in London for the weekend staying with relatives. It is so unlike Kate to wake; she's slept through the night from when she was just weeks old. *"Typical,"* I sigh to myself.

When I check on her, I realise she's fine and try everything to get her back to sleep but she's just not playing ball. She is NOT going back to sleep. She throws herself around the living room. One minute she's full of fun, giggles and play, as if it was the middle of the day and the next rubbing her tired eyes, fighting sleep, crying, and moaning. Big tears run down her red streaked cheeks.

I relentlessly try to settle her for hours and as the sun rises, she eventually collapses into a deep sleep.

Cold and exhausted I climb back into my big warm bed and instantly drift away.

What I didn't know then was that this was to be the night when everything changed.

Kate had been 18 months when we'd that weekend away in London. In the months that followed, the night-time waking carried on every single night. This was often from the early hours of the morning until the break of dawn. One sleepless night after another.

When Kate was just seven months old and her older sister Lauren almost three, I had returned to work from maternity leave earlier than intended. I'd felt a mix of sadness and guilt, along with excitement for my new role setting up a brand-new HR function within an international business.

At first Kate had settled into nursery-life well and easily adjusted. But after a few months that gradually changed. It had begun to be a battle to get her out of the car and into the nursery. And, at the end of the day it would be a battle to get her out of the nursery and into the car, strapping her into the car seat, kicking and screaming.

Every day with Kate was full of mayhem. She was a lively character from the off and kept us on our toes. A different experience from Lauren, who fell easily into routines and was a quiet and contented little girl.

Day after day, I'd fill myself with coffee, wearily dress both girls, get them to the nursery and drag myself into the office, reassuring myself that I could handle it …. I've got to handle it, there was no choice. Pushing open the office door, I'd switch on my wide awake, 'I'm on it face,' and plaster on a happy smile. Silently anxious about whether I would actually make it through the day.

Rinse and repeat. Rinse and repeat.

I was clinging to the hope that this was just a phase and wouldn't last long.

I was wrong.

These overwhelming outbursts of anger and inconsolable crying carried on.

Day after day it got worse, and I would often wonder "what the hell is going on?"

I'd noticed a few things that worried me - when she was cross, she'd bite her hand so badly, it made a huge, inflamed callus.

I felt so guilty and embarrassed when I collected her from nursery every day and the lovely team would tell me that she'd lost it and taken a lot of work to settle. Whilst on the one hand she was the funniest little girl (her saving grace), on the other, she was so difficult to manage. I felt like I was constantly on a knife-edge. One wrong move would set her off and I just didn't have the energy to deal with her.

The sleepless nights carried on and I wearily dragged myself through the first few years of her life.

Back then, it was in my nature to catastrophise things. As the situation became more intense, I'd googled all the possibilities and diagnosed a string of conditions – all of which had me in the role of full-time carer, completely broke and beaten up by my daughter – it was quite a leap I'd made back then …

I also placed a lot of pressure on myself, with high expectations in every area of my life: working hard to climb the corporate ladder, putting incredible effort into friendships, relationships, and hobbies. Nothing was ever a half measure.

Looking back, I now realise I was trying to fill a gap inside of me - that I wasn't enough. It was a lifelong story (one for another time).

Suffice to say, I was trying to be the perfect mum, with a perfect family and two perfect children. But, one of them though wasn't fitting into that mould and I would lie awake at night (with or without Kate next to me) wondering where the hell this would all end.

Her nursery was incredibly supportive and eventually we agreed that it would be best to get a professional opinion about what was going on. I'd agonised about whether to go down that road. If you cast your mind back, you'll recall that a lot of the world still had issues with disabilities.

Did I want people judging my little girl?

Did I want her labelled?

Would that screw up her life?

But the other part of me just knew that something wasn't right and that the extreme reactions and lack of sleep weren't good for her. I couldn't hide from it, no matter how much I wanted to. If I'm completely honest, part of me didn't want to find out Kate had extra needs or disabilities. Shoot me down now for feeling that way but it was the truth of how I felt at the time. It wasn't what I signed up for and was a life for other people, not me.

I had a whole 'Sound of Music' tune running through my head. You know skipping through fields, picnics, home baking. Nope, disabilities were way off plan! But once I'd had a serious word with myself and with a heavy heart, I started on a journey of seeking answers and help.

Of course, I barely told a soul, I wasn't ready to admit to anyone (including myself) what was happening. I was still clinging to that vision I had of a 'perfect life.'

After months of waiting, more sleep deprivation and endless worry, the day came that Kate and I went to see the paediatrician. I recounted all of the stories, all of my concerns and she gave me her view...

"You have a lovely, lively little girl with a wonderful imagination and should consider yourself lucky!"

So, I bleakly thanked her and trudged off out of her office, not feeling lucky but sleep deprived and stressed, fed up with not having a single moment with Kate when I could relax and stop worrying. Yes, lucky me.

That was that I thought, case closed.

Of course, part of me was relieved she was just a spirited child. No need for a label, just some better parenting, and hopefully life would settle down. It's just it didn't.

The calluses on her hand got bigger, her emotions got stronger and we experienced massive tantrums in public and private. I was constantly checking on what new life-threatening hazard she was experimenting with and couldn't take my eyes off her for a moment.

I'd got to the point where I'd learned the balance between discipline and giving in. With Lauren, the traditional 'naughty step' had worked but with Kate, I knew she'd have stayed on that step until she starved to death, rather than say sorry. There was no sorry or hug or making up. When her red mist was down, she was never giving in.

When I came to learn that she was actually angry with herself in these situations, it made me feel sad and helpless. She so desperately wanted it all to be OK, when she'd misbehaved, but she couldn't rebalance herself or get control of her emotions.

I'd often sit and just cry. Overwhelmed with this little whirlwind. On one hand feeling so much love for her and on the other feeling so desperate. Not knowing where this would all end.

I just didn't know what to do. I kept so much of this to myself for years. I couldn't have people talk about my beautiful little girl.

When she was due to start school, I knew the next set of challenges were looming. I was right and a whole new phase of stress and worry started...

Kate had the loveliest teacher and teaching assistant to

whom I will forever be grateful. School was just one problem after another. She just wouldn't do what she was told, wouldn't comply with routines or rules and wouldn't listen. School made one adjustment after another, but Kate locked herself in a cupboard, flooded the toilets, embarrassed Lauren as she pulled down her pants in school worship. It was one thing after the next.

Though school never said this, I had catastrophised the future and imagined her being expelled for her behaviour.

I was just about balancing the demands of family life, career as a HR Director (that was ramping up as we expanded our business into Europe) and coping with Kate. Somewhere in all that, I was just about coping but gradually losing myself.

After a few months in school, we all agreed the best thing to do was another referral and I had thought "Here we go again." Would I be told once more how lucky I was? That I needed a parenting class?

After many frustrating months, we made it to the front of

the referral queue. It really couldn't have come fast enough as things at school were getting worse not better.

Fortunately, we had the most amazing paediatrician who listened with care and attention. Kate calls him to this day 'Mr Chatty Man.' Within just a couple of appointments, she had a diagnosis of ADHD.

Finally - we had an answer and a treatment plan, some four years on from that first sleepless night in London, I finally felt hopeful. There was still part of me that didn't want the diagnosis as Kate was my little girl and I wanted everything to be just perfect for her. I worried what this would mean for her.

As we moved through different phases with her treatment, life got slightly easier each month.

Over the years that have followed, I very gradually shared with a few people her diagnosis. It probably wasn't a surprise to them but helped to explain some of her behaviours. It also meant that I felt that I didn't need to try so hard to control her in public.

So, where does this tale bring me to? Well, it brings me to today and where we are now.

After all that stress and worry, Kate is thriving. I couldn't have imagined back then it could have all worked out so well. She loves school, tries hard and is full of joy and fun. Everyone knows Kate for her sense of humour and whenever anyone talks about her, it generally starts with "she really makes me laugh".

So, life isn't the catastrophe I'd imagined. In fact, it is far from it. I feel blessed.

I've learned that Kate brings so much to the world. One of her gifts is that she has a unique way of looking at things, has a heart full of joy and so much love. She helps us to look at things through her eyes.

I realise that worry was something I was doing to myself, and it didn't do any good, it didn't change anything... apart from my blood pressure. It certainly wasn't helping me or helping Kate.

In fact, as I sit here now writing this, Kate's 10 and she's playing a game next to me. She's sat singing "I love you Mummy" to the tune of 'I love you baby'. When I think back to that perfect life I had imagined, I now realise there isn't such a thing, as everyone's life is unique, but this is pretty perfect for us.

Life doesn't always go to plan or work out exactly as you thought. What it can do though is end up being so much more than you ever imagined it could be.

Careers don't come in neat little boxes

Teika Marija Smits

Back in the early 1990s, when the internet as we know it today was still a far-off reality, careers advice at secondary school came in the form of a photocopied questionnaire and an interview with a bored-looking careers adviser. Still, as our frazzled teacher handed out copies of the said questionnaire to the class, a thrill of excitement ran through me. *At last!* I thought. I was going to discover my vocation! The very reason for why I was placed upon this earth. How excellent!

However, as I began to read the questions I quickly became dispirited.

Do you prefer to be indoors or outdoors? (There was only one box I could tick.)

But what if I liked to be both indoors and outdoors? I enjoyed going for walks in the woods with my family; digging around in my little patch of garden; cycling through suburbia, the wind rushing through my hair, alive to the world around me. My bike brought me independence, a foretaste of adulthood, the many journeys of my future. I was also a keen basketball player, and most of the time I practised outside, repeatedly throwing the ball against the backboard which my father had fixed to the wall of the house. The *thud, thud, thud* would reverberate through the walls and air – probably to the great annoyance of our next-door neighbours.

Then again, I was also a homebody and always thought of my home as my safe haven.

So, outdoors or indoors? I considered all the kinds of bad weather England excelled at and thought I should tick 'indoors'. But a life spent indoors, in a school classroom, an office, never seeing the daylight again or feeling the sun on my skin, would be horrifying. I ticked 'outdoors'.

Next question: *Do you prefer manual work or paperwork?* Again, there was just the one box to be ticked.

Oh crumbs! And what did they mean by manual work? Like, building work? Or making jewellery? (Surely there was a big difference between the two?) And if paperwork included writing and the kind of stuff I did at school, then that would be okay, but what if it meant filling out forms like this one? I ticked 'manual work' just to be done with the stupid query.

Another question: *Do you like working with people?* YES/NO

What?! Oh, for crying out loud. I liked some people, but not all people. And as to working with them... well it would depend on what they were like to work with. Anyway, one of my most favourite activities – reading in bed whilst chomping on chocolate, our cat curled up beside me – only really involved the one person. Me. But reading wasn't a job, was it? Glancing at my careworn teacher, I thought it was best to just circle NO.

I ploughed on through the questions, my enthusiasm ebbing away. Still, being an eternal optimist, I was sure that a careers adviser would somehow be able to magic my dream job out of all those ticks and circles I'd applied to the form.

Apparently, my ideal job was 'gardener'. *Oh*, I thought, feeling rather flat. Then again, it did make sense. After all, it was outdoors, involved manual work and dealt with very few people. But as much as I liked doing the odd bit of gardening, I didn't think it was my dream job. I must've answered the questions incorrectly. Broken the form somehow. Stupid me.

And that's one of the things I wish I'd known: that I wasn't stupid, the form was stupid. That many, many forms are incredibly stupid. That people's dreams and hopes and interests and individual peculiarities are all far too big – too diffuse and sparkly and floaty – to be crammed into one rigid box.

I also wish that when younger me was trying to figure out what career path to take, I could've had a chat with older me. Because she would've been far more helpful than that ridiculous form. She would've said, "Hey, you know what, you're going to do a little bit of everything, and for a long time it'll seem as though you can't settle on one job, but then everything will become clear, because you'll realise that there isn't just the one career; there are lots of jobs, and lots of endeavours, and lots of self-contained projects, and although some of them will be less rewarding than others, they're all going to be worthwhile. And you'll be really pleased that you've had a go at lots of different things, because one day you'll be a writer, and all these things will be useful to your writing, and they'll pop up in your stories like mushrooms, and then you'll go, *Ah, I see*, and everything will make perfect sense..."

And as well as handing me a notebook for my first attempts at writing stories, she would've told me to be mightily wary of boxes that constrain and contort.

A thing learnt along the way

Control, influence, and acceptance

Thinking about what we can control and what we can influence helps us to see where our power lies; whilst it can feel like things are happening to us, we do have control and influence. Knowing what we can do allows us to have some power in a situation that can leave us feeling powerless.

The stuff that is out of our control and our influence is where we probably spend most of our time worrying – which is futile.

Learning to accept the things we cannot control and influence, and identifying the things that we can, helps us to become more resilient and solution focused.

Focusing on what we can do and letting the rest be can be freeing.

Moving abroad was easier than I thought

Emma Scott Smith

6 July 2017 is a key date for me. It's when we moved to France permanently and, at the time, it seemed like a big deal.

With five years' hindsight, I'm not sure it was such a huge step. There have been real high points and some very low ones, of course. But, overall, we – my husband, my son and I – are glad we made the move.

But writing this essay has forced me to reflect (not something I seem to do very often) on why. Why emigrate? Why France? Why then?

So, a bit of back story to begin with. Both my husband and I had good jobs as senior managers in one of the Big Four accountancy firms. We worked hard and played hard but we were at the mercy of our employers, and we did feel as though we were on a bit of a treadmill, often working away and only catching up with each other at weekends.

Our first holiday together was to the Loire Valley in France as the first paying guests of a work colleague and her husband who had set up holiday gîtes. We loved the countryside, the feeling of space, the slower pace of life...and the wine! We returned each year and, on our third visit, the idea of doing the same thing ourselves started to germinate. So much so that, in our fourth year, we booked appointments with estate agents and found our current home.

We had recently got married; I had moved into my now husband's home and sold my own. So, we had some money in the bank and an itch to find somewhere that was *ours.* We looked at relocating in the UK but nowhere seemed to tick all the boxes.

Our French home needed to earn its keep, though, so it could provide an income when we weren't there, hence choosing somewhere that we could run as gîtes ourselves. In fact, there are now three houses on the same site; the two gîtes were here from the outset but we converted a small barn into our home between 2014 and 2016. That way, we could come and go as we liked and still earn an income from holidaymakers. Friends did the cleaning, garden ~~taming~~ maintenance, and the 'meet and greets', while I looked after bookings and dealt with queries from afar.

I was happy to have a holiday home. I also love travel and exploring new places, but could I move for good? Leave friends and family, not to mention the certainty and security?

My husband says he always felt he'd like to have three careers. After university, he'd joined the Royal Hong Kong Police Force. After 13 years there, rising to the rank of Superintendent, he moved back to the UK as a forensic accountant and that's how we met. But there was a yearning in him to do something else...and a fearlessness I envied about doing that in a different country.

Yet, somewhere along the line, we decided to take the plunge and move abroad permanently. Before our son arrived in 2013, we might have changed to a work pattern that allowed us to spend more time in France. Indeed, since COVID-19, many organisations have embraced hybrid working, so perhaps it would not have been such a stretch to think of working 'from home' – no-one else needed to know which home, after all.

But with our son to consider, it felt fairer to him to move so that he could start school in France, rather than start in the UK and have the upheaval of leaving friends and understanding a new education system.

His first day at school will remain etched in my mind. We'd shown him where the school was and talked with him about it during the summer but none of us was fluent in French.

We explained he wouldn't understand what was going on at first, and suggested he just copy what the other children were doing. But when we dropped him off in his classroom only knowing the French for 'yes', 'no', 'my name is...', and 'where are the toilets?', I think we can be forgiven for coming home and having a stiff drink!

Since then, he's thrived. He's fluent for his age and has an accent to die for and we are so very proud of him.

In contrast, although I did well at French at school and have a good memory, it's still a long time ago. So, every day is a learning day. Progress is not as fast as I'd like. But it is still progress. I've realised that language is contextual: we started with learning 'building French' as we tried to converse with builders and make sense of their invoices. Our neighbour – a stonemason who did much of our barn renovation work – joked that the first objective of our project was for us to learn French; the second was to create a home. Then came 'school French' as I grappled with the system, helped my son with his homework and attended parents' evenings. This was followed by 'medical French' when I was admitted to Saumur hospital in 2018 with tuberculosis – definitely one of the low points.

I thought I'd be able to converse with patients and nurses but, being infectious, I was in a room on my own. Thank goodness for smartphones so I had human contact!

After 12 days in isolation, I was allowed out but had to remain in quarantine for six weeks (fortunately I could live in our gîte), follow an eight-month course of antibiotics and wear a mask in public. Oh yes, I was a trailblazer on the mask front, long before anyone had heard of COVID!

We've also had to get into the health and tax systems. The French do love their bureaucracy. It's often easier meeting face-to-face and being able to gesture than trying to discuss issues over the phone. I've even been known to take a big French-English dictionary with me just in case there's no WiFi and, therefore, no Google Translate to help me out. And, when something is resolved, I punch the air with delight – even the little wins feel momentous.

Brexit put a spanner in the works, of course, but it didn't derail our plans. After all, you could move abroad before the UK joined the EU. It's just harder now without freedom of movement. With the help of an advisor, appropriately called 'The Fixer', we got our medical cards (care is not all free at the point of delivery here) and, finally, our residency cards. So, we're now legal. They were just more bumps in the road along the way.

I still work as an independent training consultant. I used to travel back to the UK about twice a month to run training courses. As an extrovert, this gave me the buzz of city life and engaging with others, while my husband (an introvert) enjoyed a bit of peace and quiet. When the first COVID lockdown happened, companies understandably cancelled their training, so I had no work coming in. We weren't allowed to open our gîtes either, so our financial situation seemed bleak.

Strangely, I felt far less worried than I thought I might because the situation was out of my control. Even though we have plenty of garden here, we still went 'off site' as a family to walk the dog each day, armed with our 'attestations' showing our name and address to ensure we didn't venture further than the permitted one kilometre from home. The combination of family time, fresh air, and exercise was good for bonding and mental health. To be fair, we're so rural I'd have been surprised if anyone official had come to check up on us.

Once the first lockdown ended, we were lucky to have a summer season full of French guests who still wanted a holiday. They couldn't travel abroad either but as one group, who had been locked down in a city only 40 minutes away, put it, "we just need to exhale."

Also, companies soon realised they still needed to train their staff, even though many were working remotely. So, I embraced Zoom and converted the courses I run to online versions. I wonder if I'll ever get back to presenting in a 'classroom'. I specialise in business writing training which, I've discovered, lends itself well to the virtual environment. In fact, in some ways it's better as participants can share their screens and we can discuss and edit their live documents in real time.

Our move to France means we spend more time together as a family, experience another culture and are more in control of what we do.

The recipe for survival seems to be perseverance, resilience, and dealing with challenges head on, while not expecting things to be the same as in the UK.

After all, where's the fun in that?

Should I?

How often do we tell ourselves what we should – or shouldn't – be doing?

Sometimes, with good cause: to keep ourselves safe, to evade possible risks, to avoid causing ourselves harm, to do the right thing.

But all too often, that little word is used to self-sabotage.

Should – or shouldn't – is full of expectation and judgement. We set ourselves up with the use of 'should' – and when we fall below these expectations – expectations we possibly may not even really desire or aspire to – we find ourselves wracked with guilt and disappointment. We use 'should' to set standards for ourselves, and when we don't achieve them, we feel that we have failed. It can be utterly miserable.

And, how much are we using 'should' as a barrier to hold us back from following our dreams?

We can look out for should, notice when we're telling ourselves what we should and shouldn't be doing. Recognise it. And then challenge it.

- *Is this 'should' helpful or keeping me safe?*

- *If not, what is it that I really want instead?*

- *Is this should keeping me from the things that I want?*

- *What would I do if I wasn't telling myself what I should be doing?*

How to overcome imposter syndrome

Vicki Haverson

Feeling that you're not intelligent, capable, creative, or good enough, despite your achievements.

Feeling that you are just winging it, that you're a fraud and one day you're going to get found out.

Feeling that you don't know enough or deserve to be in a room with all these other people who seem more experienced and capable than you are.

Feeling that you've just been lucky when you get that job, receive a promotion or a pay rise.

I wish I'd known that these feelings are surprisingly common for many of us. That it wasn't just me feeling this way and that imposter syndrome exists amongst us everywhere.

When I started researching imposter syndrome I found myself in the company of at least 70 per cent of people, according to the journal of behavioural science.

When you suffer from imposter syndrome you might wonder, like me for a long time, "how can I fit it here and belong?" When you look around you feel different. Perhaps you are quieter, more considered, and reflective whilst others around you seem more energetic, faster paced and seemingly comfortable speaking up. It can make you overly self-critical and unable to recognise the bits that make you good.

Part of the challenge is we are all predisposed from a young age to fixate on what we don't do well. Maybe, like me, you brought home a report card from school with some good grades and one or two not so good ones. My not so good one was Maths. I just never got it and always had a D. My parents fixated on my grade, insisting I wouldn't get anywhere in life without it.

Hours and hours of effort and extra tuition after school and at weekends went into Maths, to the point I was convinced I might even end up with an A. Yet I just scraped a C.

My Maths experience plagued me with self-doubt about my intelligence. It also drained me because I was focusing on a weakness, which meant I only marginally improved and the subjects that I was good at suffered as I neglected them. I discovered much later that this happens to two thirds of children whose parents focus on the poor grades when they bring home their report cards.

So the feelings we develop about being an imposter start at a young age. It can make us exaggerate and fixate on our weaknesses and make us doubt ourselves and our decisions. It gets in the way of things like having challenging conversations – one of the things we can find hard to do at home and in our workplaces – because you worry these conversations might expose you. It can encourage us to withdraw or avoid the moments we really need to be stepping into.

What's rather ironic is that people with imposter syndrome are often reflective, conscientious, and concerned about delivering for the organisations they work for and taking care of their relationships. Which means we really need to find ways to support each other and normalise these feelings by talking about them and sharing our experiences.

There are four things that I have found that have helped me personally to navigate my own feelings of Imposter Syndrome.

Know your strengths

If you don't know yourself and appreciate your strengths and know that it's ok to have weaknesses – because we all have them – then your experience of feedback isn't going to be a good one. It's going to leave you in fear instead of being something you can take in your stride.

My imposter syndrome is often triggered by fear of feedback. An email after a meeting – *what are they going to say? Have they found me out? What went wrong? A meeting request – it's going to be bad feedback, they're going to fire me.* Needing to return a call. *What do they need to speak to me about? Who have I upset? What did I do wrong?*

When you can identify your strengths and access the

stories of your successes, it is easier to remove that voice of doubt. Which makes it harder for your imposter to show up.

Discovering my strengths through a tool called Clifton Strengths was life changing for me. It helped me to own and build my confidence around who I am and the things I do well and let go of the things that I don't so I could get help where I needed it.

When you know your strengths it also helps you understand what you need to be at your best and what might trigger you. For example, one of my Clifton Strengths is Input — I love to research and gather information. I like to know stuff about the subjects that really interest me. Not knowing can trigger me into feeling like an imposter and spiral me into thinking that I look like I don't know what I'm talking about, or that I *should* know more about this. And should words are dangerous because they are an active form of self-criticism that create anxiety and stress.

Which brings me onto the second thing you can do about imposter syndrome:

Admit what you don't know

My first job was buying car parts for a car manufacturer. I remember sitting in a meeting about a new project with someone senior who talked in technical terms and acronyms. I'd only been in the job a couple of months and I felt sick, writing notes as fast as I could. I was convinced I was going to lose my job as I didn't understand a word he was saying, which felt like a much better option than admitting I didn't know what he was talking about. I was so relieved when someone else in the meeting said they weren't familiar with these terms and could they explain them.

I've sat there wondering about something in a meeting many times over the years, only to find someone else asks the very questions I want to, or it turns out afterwards they didn't understand it either. A way to combat this is to accept that we are not experts in *anything.* Getting out of the mindset of "I need to know the answers and the knowledge and the right way to do this" and instead step into curiosity with myself and others has made a massive difference.

Ask for help

Most of us are much better at giving than asking for help. Help can feel uncomfortable and we can judge ourselves for asking for it. When we have imposter syndrome, we worry what people will think.

Just as we have strengths, we all have weaknesses. I like to think of our strengths as an opportunity for us to help others and our weaknesses are an opportunity for others to help us.

We can get help when we recognise those imposter feelings and talk about them. Remembering we're not the only person that feels this way and there is nothing like talking to someone about your feelings who has earned the right to hear them.

Asking for help is sharing your vulnerability. When you are vulnerable it makes you brave and it also really annoys your imposter syndrome because it loses its power. When it comes to imposter syndrome, we are not alone and we need to find ways to normalise rather than label it.

Let go of perfectionism

People that struggle with imposter syndrome often have really high expectations of themselves to a level of perfection that are cemented in childhood. Many of us were raised for achievement and performance, be it our grades, following rules, our appearance or pleasing other people.

Perfectionism can creep up and paralyse me if I'm not careful. It can manifest itself as procrastination because I worry the work, the decision, the conversation won't be good enough, so I put it off. Or negative self-talk after a decision, an event or conversation takes place leading to feelings of fear and anxiety.

Perfectionism is often focused on others. *"What will they think, say, or do?"* We look for approval and acceptance from others. It's a heavy weight that we carry around with us. What I've learnt is that perfectionism isn't obtainable and it only ever leads to disappointment.

If we instead change the frame within which we think about it to 'how can I improve' it becomes healthy and self-focused.

Perfectionism self-talk looks like: You could have done that better. It wasn't good enough.

Healthy self-talk: It didn't go the way I hoped and I learnt a lot about what I might do differently next time I'm faced with a similar situation.

In the research I've done Brené Brown says it best in her brilliant book 'The Gifts of Imperfection'.

"The most difficult part of our stories is often what we bring to them — what we make up about who we are and how we are perceived by others. Yes, maybe we failed or screwed up a project, but what makes that story so painful is what we tell ourselves about our own self-worth and value. Because the truth is that no one belongs here more than you."

Being me is actually, really okay

Lisa Dymond

My most profound memory and one that shaped my being as I muddled my way through life was me, 12 years old, as I returned home from school early to be with my grandmother, my beautiful everything, my Mo-Mo as she passed away. Around that same formative earth-shattering time my parents' marriage ended and I could not have felt more alone.

As an only child moving counties and schools, leaving my friends behind, I had always felt a sense of being on my own. Yes, at times I was lonely and yes at times I felt sad and by the age of 12, looking back I had realised that the people and relationships that had made me feel safe and secure had gone. Bowlby's (1977) attachment theory acknowledges that as people we need to have strong emotional bonds and that strong emotional reactions can happen when these are threatened or broken and that this comes from our need for security and safety.

It's funny then how hard some of us feel we have to try to be liked, to be loved, to be recognised, to be wanted and I have tried my whole life to be these things to people and feel these things from people.

Do you want to know me? Be my friend? I never had a large friendship circle, nor do I think I wanted one, but I always wanted (and still do) to be liked. Thankfully, I do have the absolute best few friends and I value them wholeheartedly. You see I'm fiercely loyal, some might say I set my expectations of other people's behaviours and actions high, and I think that comes from knowing the pain of being broken.

As I've grown, I've realised that strength comes from learning, don't ever stop learning. I'm a mental health nurse and consider myself to have a good career and one that I love. This field gripped me and captured my spirit and I applied myself to higher education!

I have built a career I love out of helping others, but as the beautiful by-product I have helped myself.

Not always knowing and not always realising, but with the benefit of reflecting on my past, my experiences and knowing that everything happens for a reason, even if at the time we don't know what that reason is. I assure you, you will.

So, what have I learnt along my way? Well, being alone is ok and being lonely from time to time is ok too. I believe for me this has given me the ability to reflect on myself and given me the confidence not to compare myself to others (too much) - don't do that, it's not healthy or realistic.

It's also ok to be individual, be you, and know your worth.

But how do we as women achieve that?

Do something you love, not just for work, but whenever you can and do it for yourself, to be proud of all your achievements. I don't mean be selfish, kindness goes a long way too and will serve you well, be kind. It'll also boost your mood.

Build positive relationships and learn to be assertive, by that I mean learn the ability to confidently communicate what you want or need while also respecting the needs of others.

Be physically active, exercise and look after your body. Physical and mental health are equally important and go hand in hand, you and your body are going to be with each other for hopefully a long time. Respect both.

I've talked a bit about reflection and having the ability to look back and learn, but don't get lost in the past, pay attention to the present moment too.

It can be all too easy to rush around without stopping to notice what is going on inside and outside of ourselves. If you don't know what mindfulness is I suggest you look into it, it can help us be more aware and understand ourselves better.

So, to conclude with the piece of learning, my knowledge, my life learnt wisdom that I want to pass on to you, is that it's actually really okay being you, even when perhaps you don't feel like it is. Sense is what you make of it, even if it doesn't make any sense.

It's ok being you, so take care and value yourself and your wellbeing.

The worst things can lead onto the best path

Ronda Jackson

Although sometimes I wish I had known things, I feel grateful for the lessons which I have learned in the process.

I could say I wish I had known not to take a particular job that was offered to me when I was about 30. I didn't know that taking that job would be a big turning point in my life. I hated that job. I realised really quickly after starting that I was going to hate that job.

That job made me ill. The pressure of what was expected of me every day and the working environment soon resulted me coming home from work and crying most days. I used to dread going to work. My stomach would get tied in a knot as I would approach the building and the smell of the place made me feel like I was going to have a panic attack. Sometimes I did have panic attacks. I don't really know why this job affected me so badly. I don't know why I tried so hard to do a good job but it was one of those jobs where I was never going to be good enough and I just strived harder and harder to get it all done and make the boss proud. I was pushed to breaking point.

I had never had panic attacks before or sleepless nights worrying about a job.

Before this happened to me I could never really understand when people used to talk about panic attacks I think I always thought it was something people did to get attention.

When it started happening to me it was scary. I was scared. I felt more and more out of control as the time working there went on.

Then my mum got cancer. Things went from bad to worse.

On top of that I suffered a miscarriage.

Suddenly it felt like life was too short to go to a job every day that made me feel ill.

So I left.

I had no job, a sick mum, and a mortgage to pay. I also had plans for starting a family but I didn't feel healthy or strong.

I left the job and I knew I needed to get better.

I decided I was going to start my own business. I was going to do what I do but on a self-employed basis so that's what I did.

Within three months I was earning the same as before and I was able to take every Friday off to take my mum for radiotherapy.

My mum recovered. And I am pleased to say has stayed cancer free ever since.

I started my own business which I still run today 15 years on.

That time and that job has taught me so much. It's taught me how important mental health is. How to recognise the symptoms and to get on top of things before they spiral out of control. It taught me never to let a job make me ill again.

It's also taught me what sort of business owner I want to be what sort of boss I want to be and how to value the people that work for me. None of these lessons I would have learned if I had not had that awful experience.

There is a saying that rock bottom will teach you lessons that mountain tops never will. Sometimes the thing that seems like the worst thing can lead you to the path of the best thing that's about to happen. I wish I had known that.

A thing learnt along the way

An attitude of gratitude

Taking a moment to notice the good stuff in our lives is so good for us. It helps us feel good, it builds up our resilience, and the more we do it, the more things we notice.

One way you can build your attitude of gratitude is by keeping a journal. Write down the good things from each day – and keep writing until you fill the page. And it doesn't have to be big stuff. It could be things like someone making you a cup of tea, or finding a good parking spot, or a kind word. It could be everyday things that become magical things once you stop and recognise them.

Or you could do it as a family. Grab a jar and each member writes down a good thing from their day every evening.

What's more, you can get to notice the good thing twice – once when you write it down, and again when you revisit and read it back.

Of course, it can be really hard to notice the good stuff when things are tough. But that's when we need to do it even more – that's when we need the positives to uplift us.

There really is an abundance of things to be grateful for. We just need to stop and look.

My mind is magic

Daisy Reynolds

When I look back on my life so far, it saddens me to know that I have spent far too long worrying about what other people think about me. As a teenager, a student at university, throughout my twenties navigating the world of work and relationships, and now in my thirties as a married mum of two, there have always been feelings of self-doubt that have come to the surface.

Over the past few years, I have realised that working on my mindset leads to positive things. I have learnt that when negative thought patterns arise, I must take control, and change my way of thinking. How I do this is by spending time doing things that make me feel happier and uplifted. This could be in the form of reading a great book ('The Secret' by Rhonda Byrne is a book everyone should read!), listening to a podcast, dancing to my favourite songs, or chatting and laughing with a friend. Life is too short to worry and be consumed with anxiety. Here are a few lessons I have learnt so far.

Practice gratitude everyday whilst in the 'pursuit of happiness'

I think sometimes we can think about what we want so much, the bigger house, the flashy car, the larger salary that we forget to be grateful for the things we already have. Never lose sight of what's important. By simply writing down a few things you are grateful for in the morning and just before you go to sleep, means you are waking up and ending the day with gratitude.

Forgive yourself for past mistakes

Every single person on the planet makes mistakes, it's what makes us human. What matters is that we learn from them and forgive ourselves in the process. I have made plenty of errors in judgement, but life is a journey of self-discovery and everything that has happened in my life so far has made me the person who I am today.

You will never be able to please everybody

This is something that is worth understanding early on in life. You will never please everyone, so you just have be true to yourself and what you believe in. You may not always be popular because of it, but that's ok. Don't be afraid to lose people. Be afraid of losing yourself by trying to please everyone around you.

Nobody is going to come and make your dreams happen

The only person that is in control of your life is you. If you have a dream or goal, then it's up to you to make it happen. If you want something start today and do it for you. Never stop believing in your dreams. If you don't believe you'll get there, then who else will?

Nobody is entitled to a relationship with you

You can choose who you let into your life and it's really important to choose your circle wisely. People don't get an automatic right to have a relationship with you. Whether it's a family member or friend, don't be afraid to cut people out of your life if they're making you feel sad. Your spirit and energy are precious, so it's essential that you're careful with them.

Sleep is everything

Getting a good night's sleep every day is essential for

keeping your energy and mood high. When I became a mum, nobody could have warned me about how much of a killer sleep deprivation truly is. It literally affects everything – your mindset, your emotional stability, your focus, your relationships, your energy, and your ability to make smart choices when it comes to exercise and food. Don't underestimate the power of sleep and how it makes you function.

Always be kind

Kindness doesn't cost a thing. Think how one nice comment from a stranger would make you feel. Spread the love and smile. It will instantly raise your vibrations, make somebody else's day better, and you will go to sleep in the knowledge that you've been a kind a thoughtful person that day.

Be mindful of what you consume

What we consume makes a massive difference to our mindset. For example, consuming too much alcohol can make us feel anxious and vulnerable the next day. Eating the wrong types of foods can make us unmotivated and sluggish. Watching the news or a negative documentary can zap us of our energy and positivity. Being mindful of what your body and mind is consuming every day is the key to a happy life.

Decide what kind of day you'll have

When you wake up in the morning, you literally have the choice to decide you're going to have a great day. If you want to be happy and positive, be happy and positive on purpose. Keep your thoughts, energy, experiences, and vibrations high all day.

Remind yourself of how amazing you are

Once you realise your worth, you will start to attract beautiful things into your life. It all starts with you. You have to *believe* you are worthy of all the good things in your life. Remember, you are unique. There is only one of you in the entire universe.

A thing learnt along the way

Give yourself space to think

How often do we give ourselves space to reflect, to consider, to formulate ideas, to dream, to visualise, to....think? How often do we proactively and practically set aside our precious time to do just that?

So often we get embroiled in task and work and life admin that we leave few gaps for our brains to just do its magic.

Because that's what happens when we give ourselves space and time – and permission, perhaps most importantly of all – to think. Magic happens. We find ourselves able to travel in directions previously unknown, to uncover nuggets of gold we might never had expected, and find solutions to problems that we didn't know we had up our sleeves.

It is always ok to ask for help

Haley Minns

I cast my mind back to November 2014 and I had just found out I was pregnant. It was a happy time but also one tinged with an overriding feeling of worry! Like many, I had previously suffered a miscarriage (my first was 2013) and so it was very difficult to get too excited about something I had expected to come to an end.

This time though, I was lucky and I made it through to 36 weeks and six days and my perfect son was born. My labour was amazing and I had a healthy, beautiful baby boy. I couldn't believe he was real and he was mine. I was happy, I had everything I wanted and I really felt I was going to be a great mum.

After a week in hospital with some breast-feeding issues and a baby with jaundice, we went home and the weeks ticked on. We went through, what I now know as 'normal', highs and lows of having a newborn baby. New challenges every day and a life that was totally different to what we had known. Looking back, I remember feeling worried all the time, anxious about the baby and if what I was doing was right and I only felt some relief from this when my mum was with me. She had two children so in my mind she knew what she was doing.

It was a few weeks on (time frames are difficult to remember now) and one night at home with my husband I was crying uncontrollably and I couldn't stop. Nothing specific had caused it and it must have been after almost an hour of him asking me what was wrong that I was finally able to get the words out to tell him "I think I'm depressed." Getting those words to come out of my mouth was so ridiculously hard, I knew once they had been said I couldn't take them back and I felt like such a huge failure, to my son, my husband, my family, and to myself.

But I knew, I knew I didn't feel right, I knew the worry was out of control, I knew I shouldn't feel how I did. More than anything I knew that I had to ask for help for the sake of my son.

What came next was a few weeks of asking for help.

Asking and asking and asking. I don't know how but I knew I had post-natal depression, I knew how I felt and I knew that the main thing that was going to make me better was medication. What I didn't know then was that it was going to be a quick or easy process and I would need to keep asking for help until I felt like me again.

I went to so many doctors' appointments to ask for help, not an easy process when leaving the baby makes you feel anxious, taking the baby out makes you feel anxious, phoning for an appointment makes you feel anxious, even attempting to shower seems impossible. Then came the referrals, workshops, support workers, and anxiety medication that knocked me out cold and finally the medication that eventually made me feel like me again – still a worrier but under control worry.

Looking back at this time in my life I was certainly not myself but even in the depressed state I was in I kept asking for the help I knew I needed. I know that I did this because of the circumstances I was in - I wanted to be better for the sake of my baby. I never failed to bond with him but the overwhelming worry and sadness I felt I knew

I had to deal with so I could give him the best I could.

So what did I wish I had known?

I asked for help with my depression, but what I do wish is that I had known that this is ok to do. I felt embarrassed about the situation I was in, like a failure and like it was my fault. I know now that this was wrong.

It is always ok to ask for help if you need it, in any situation. It might not be a mental health issue, it might be something really small and it is still ok to ask for help. There will always be someone who cares, who understands, who has the tools or can just be there.

I am good enough

Jacqueline Fry

I wish I had known that I was good enough.

As a child you are encouraged to learn and take advantage of the opportunities to develop that come your way. I loved school, I love to learn new things. I want to understand how and why things happen as they do. I'm not intellectual, philosophical debates are not my thing. General knowledge of what makes the world turn is my limit.

Primary school in the seventies was full of basic development, boys and girls were equal and given the same opportunities. Then the rules changed and we were no longer able to sit exams to determine what level of education we would get at secondary school, a selection system was introduced which was supposed to be better. For me it failed; classes were just sent to either high school or grammar school. There was no option for everyone else from age ten, my path was set by the system.

A lot of my friends when into the high school system and I went into secondary modern. They had a different journey through education, they were schooled in sitting exams and for 'O'levels from the start.

At age 11 doors were already being closed, social circles were determined, the chances of going on to university were reduced simply because we were not taught in the same way. Subjects were gender specific, sciences were restricted. We could go on a day release to the local college to take typing but not mechanics that was for the boys. We were not allowed to take woodwork or metalwork, we could only take needlecraft or domestic science.

The school you went to determined the networking, there was even a divide between the secondary modern system of schools, you simply didn't mix. In the final two years of secondary the rules changed again and we were in mixed classes with the boys. In the final year change came again and comprehensive education was brought in. Now we were mixed with the high school and able to take 'O' levels. All of which was too late.

So following the path set out for me in life, I worked, I married, I had children. Then came the divorce.

At age 42, as a single parent with two children, I was not going to let myself fall. I had a limited social life being a working mum so I turned back to education and found the Open University. Seven long years later I got my honours degree. I had two well-grounded children and the education behind me that I felt I had missed out on.

With the education came the opportunities, that alongside life learning has taught me that I did have it in me. Circumstances out of my control had held me back. But I am and always was good enough. Life is about knowing your worth and knowing that you can achieve what you want.

A thing learnt along the way

Recognising intent and input

We tend to measure our success on the outcomes of what we do. But the problem with that is that we so often overlook and disregard our input and intent - the huge efforts we put into the things that we do.

So when things go wrong, when we don't get the outcomes we want, we can find ourselves affected by negative emotions.

And so, actively recognising that we can control what we put in – our input and intent – and not the outcomes will help to stop us being that person, wide awake at 3am, pondering outcomes that were far from desired.

"I did everything I could," and "I had the best of intentions," are two statements that can remind us of that fact.

Life is too short to not do the things that make you happy

Suzanna Wood

And these are the things that I've learnt make me happy:

Family should always come first

When the Covid pandemic hit and we went into lockdown, I started to work from home. With children at primary school, I was juggling home schooling and working full time but I felt like I had so much more time. I could be there when my girls woke up in the morning, we could have breakfast together, go for a walk at the end of the day and I could still focus and do my job well.

Once the world started to go back to normal, I knew that I wanted an element of homeworking so that I could take my girls to school and be there when they got home. I wanted to be around for them more and it's now something that matters when I look at a new career opportunity, it's something I discuss openly. Most employers now embrace it and I wish I'd discussed it sooner. My children will only be young once and I don't want to miss the chance to be there.

Being happy in the workplace

I've worked in many different roles and organisations in my career in housing and I've loved most of them. One role just didn't feel right, I didn't feel that I could make a difference there, I was working long hours and my health started to suffer. I wish I'd known sooner that it was ok to move on and look for a new opportunity without feeling like a failure. I wasted a lot of time feeling miserable and could have changed my situation much quicker.

How a coach can change your outlook

I have worked with an amazing coach for a number of years, it started when I was looking for a new opportunity and she came along and helped me evaluate what I had achieved, think objectively about what I wanted and where I wanted to be and gave me a much-needed boost of energy and confidence. I wish I'd met her sooner in my career. Thank you Sarah, you are worth your weight in gold!

Imposter Syndrome

I didn't realise how many people struggle with this and don't talk about it. I attended an amazing training session a few years ago with an inspiring lady called Gemma who helped me find tools to banish my imposter when she appears. I wish this was something taught in schools or universities as it would have helped me in my early career to find my true potential.

Find your tribe

Good friends and colleagues are so important, but you don't need to be friends with everyone. Find people that love and support you for being you. I wish I'd accepted this sooner.

Exercise

Makes me happy. Some days it feels really tough but once I've pulled on my trainers and been for a long run, I feel so much happier. Wish I'd discovered it sooner in life.

Falling in love

And finding the right person is so tricky, it took me a while to find the right match. My husband is my biggest cheerleader, he supports me after a tough day, encourages me when needed and loves me unconditionally. I wish I'd met him sooner in life.

Life is too short, do the things you love, surround yourself with like-minded people you feel comfortable with and never regret anything that made you smile.

Taking a risk for love was worth it

Fiona Tait

Do I regret making that decision to be with him after his accident in 2003 when lots of people warned me not to rekindle our relationship. The answer is no. Would I do it all again? Yes.

His accident happened in October 2003, and I still remember that fateful phone call that would turn my life upside down. My parents sitting me down and explaining that he was in hospital in Melbourne – halfway round the world. The next few days, weeks were an emotional whirlwind as I anxiously waited to see if he would survive. On life support, in a coma with little brain activity. His dad flew out to be with him. I waited helplessly for phone call updates from his devastated best friend having witnessed the accident.

Miraculously he survived. A born fighter or just pure stubborn defying the odds of the Glasgow coma readings!

The joy of knowing that he had woken up and asked,

"where's that girl?" Yes, the brain injury had caused immense irreparable damage, but my heart soared because he remembered me despite not being able to say my name. The first phone call was short but momentous. His constant repeating "are you good?" didn't matter because he was alive and speaking.

Seven months later I flew out to Melbourne. Recently out of a rehab hospital he was living with his best friend. Concerned and well-intentioned family and friends advised me not to get my hopes and his hopes up and that resuming a relationship was a huge commitment. I nodded and assured them all that I just needed to see him. We would be friends.

Jet-lagged, and after what seemed like the longest taxi journey, I arrived at his door. Tentatively I rang the bell. Was I prepared for who was behind the door? There was no denying it was a shock. He was thin and his very visible scar stood out on his shaved head. Huge, frightened eyes stared at me not quite believing I was there on his doorstep. His vulnerability hit me and the love that had never gone away came flooding back washing over me like a tidal wave. Looking back that was probably the moment that I knew I was in it for the long haul no matter what. Blinded by young love when anything seems possible.

He would stay in Melbourne for the next four years receiving rehab, from learning to walk and coping with navigating his way round due to sight problems. Weekly speech therapy and basically supporting him to live independently. Helping him adapt and cope with his disabilities. Supported by his dad, his best friend and myself we tried to help him. His stubbornness and resilience were amazing. His determination to get better and be 'normal' were what drove him in the early days. In between teacher training and becoming a teacher I would fly out to be with him. Our days would be spent frequenting Melbourne coffee shops a habit he has not lost – he loves a coffee! I would also do admin for him; since he had lost the ability to read and write, numbers were a problem, and his verbal dysphasia was a constant source of frustration for him.

In the early days of his recovery, I marvelled at how he

would try his hardest to communicate and get his meaning across. Like a complex game of charades, I became good at guessing what he meant; for example, when he spoke of the hair on the face he meant a beard.

The dark days came. As the doctors had advised a brain injury is complex and recovery an unknown quantity, the brain makes new connections and he had made amazing progress, but it became clear that his days being able to work as a TV producer were long gone. Accepting this took time. He refused to talk to psychologists and pretended he was ok. I was sheltered by some of this as I felt like I was living two lives. One working in the UK, the other being the girlfriend visiting in Melbourne. Finally on a visit I persuaded him that he needed to talk to someone. It was heartbreaking listening to him confide in the therapist that he had contemplated suicide. One of the only reasons stopping him going through with it was me. It was hard not to cry. In retrospect it was a hell of a thing to listen to and a weight of responsibility on my shoulders. Did I fully comprehend that? Not at the time. All I wanted to do was make sure he was ok.

In 2007 he arrived back in the UK and moved in with me. This new chapter was not without challenges. Firstly, he didn't know many people, he was worried about speaking to people because of his speech and saying the wrong word. I was aware that I was not around for him all the time and felt guilty for the number of hours he was on his own, juggling a full-time job and helping him settle was at times stressful. It felt like we were starting all over again with medical appointments and trying to get him some support. The honeymoon period of visiting him in Australia was over. I was aware that when I was tired, I lacked patience to understand what he wanted to say. I didn't just want to be his carer I also wanted to be his girlfriend. Having the support of family and friends nearby helped immensely in the early days of life back in the U.K. While he could have easily sunk into a depression, he found ways to fill his days. Cooking for me, making pizzas became his obsession for a while. He found ways round obstacles and barriers due to his disability. For example, an avid reader before his brain injury he now listens to audio books. He is an amazing, resilient man and an optimist. He created new opportunities becoming a wedding videographer. The difficult part was helping him to run his business. It did put a strain on our relationship as he relied on me to email clients and do his admin. I wanted to help him but sometimes his communication difficulties would cause misunderstandings and he would become frustrated with situations. It was sometimes easy for me to forget that he had so many difficulties. Tiredness and lack of patience played a part. Sometimes you need reminding of why you love someone.

We spend a lot of time together more than most couples. I have realised that my coping mechanism is seeing friends; having space away from him makes me appreciate him more. He also likes to feel like he can do things on his own. He does not like to be referred to as disabled. He hardly ever admits when things are too hard for him. He pretends and masks his difficulties with others. I worry about him being socially isolated. But he has this amazing warmth and ability to chat to anyone. He is a sociable character. The challenges are hard because he cannot cope with large groups of people, when the conversations flow too quickly and topics change. He is much better in small groups and one to one. Strangers probably think he is eccentric in the way he talks, but he can get his meaning across. I am protective of him in new situations, and I have realised that I will never stop worrying about him. His memory problems have caused endless rows and situations. He always forgets his phone or doesn't answer it. But the important thing is that after the drama, we can joke and laugh about it.

So yes in 2003 I did have the choice. I made my decision to be with him. It's hard work, we have our ups and downs but there is never a dull moment. He is an amazing father to our two children he can give them his undivided attention. I'm jealous of his relaxed attitude and calm manner but there again he's not me having to juggle four people's diaries. He gets to be the fun one, I get to be the nag, the one that runs round bugging them about homework, the glorified taxi driver. I did want someone to take care of me and he does in his own way. But I know I will be the one taking care of him, let's hope for a long time yet. I took a risk for love. And it has been worth it.

Fear is a choice

Michelle Atkinson

For years I dreamed of someday having my own business, setting myself up as a professional coach, to be more and do more of what I love. I dreamed of doing work with a diverse and broad reach and a varied portfolio of clients. With a mission in my heart to help people occupy the space in their lives they have the human potential to fill, I observed with admiration those in the coaching and development profession who had 'made it' by definition of them doing more of what they love day to day and loving what they do. I looked to them for inspiration, I learned from them and was motivated and energised by doing so. I worked hard throughout my career building my skills and gaining knowledge and experience to help me get to my 'someday' and where I wanted to be. A dream I had previously shared with my manager at the time. I studied, and studied and did even more study, attending every relevant training course and gaining practical experience. I wanted to make sure I had the knowledge, skills, credentials, and credibility to progress my dreams of one day, when I grew up, being my own boss at the head of my own successful coaching company.

With professional coaching accreditations and certificates, advanced coaching training and all the experience I was grateful to gain throughout my 25-year career spanning roles in fast paced, complex, regularly changing corporate environments, I had everything I needed as a highly trained and experienced coach in good standing to pursue my 'some day'. Despite this, and despite being told I was more than ready, I found myself dancing between the fear of changing everything, stepping out of a successful career, and venturing into my own business and the hesitation to leap into the opportunity that was in front of me, calling me forward to a place centred around my purpose to help others thrive. I was stuck in the dance. I wish I had remembered that fear was a choice.

Inspiration is everywhere if you're open to it and it can be found in the most surprising of places. I'm minded of a quote from the movie Karate Kid 3 when Mr Miyagi said to Daniel, his karate student, during the final tournament where he was injured: "It's ok to lose to opponent, it's never ok to lose to fear". Daniel was also encouraged to 'stay focused' as Mr Miyagi told him "your best karate is still inside you, now it's time to let it out". It was a chance moment of turning on the TV a few minutes before that scene unfolded. I remember thinking how very profound that was to hear. Some would say, I heard what I needed to hear at just the right time I needed to hear it! Others would say it was a pure coincidence. Either way, it moved something in me and with the voices of my supporters and Mr Miyagi's words echoing through my mind, I had to try. My best life was still in me and I had to let my best life out to see what I could become. I'd been talking about my someday, one day dream, and was allowing fear to make procrastination a comfortable place to hang out. I was allowing fear to keep me stuck.

An enjoyable career, deep investment in the people I worked with and a loyalty for the organisation made it all the harder to hand in my notice and resign from my job. It took me two attempts to leave and when I finally chose the courage to resign for the second time, it was a leader

I worked with who recognised that this time I was moving towards something great and deeply purpose-led rather than away from a job or an organisation and therefore any attempts to convince me to stay would be futile. A pivotal conversation that unlocked the procrastination I had come to know and feel safe in. A shared realisation that this was the right risk to take and that I needed to give it a go and fulfil my potential. During moments of change I often hear people say "when the time is right". I have learned that the time is right when you say it is. I had and still have a brilliant support network to help me on my way and friends and family that really stepped up with heaps of encouragement to "go for it". I am wholeheartedly grateful to every brilliantly unique one of them for every chat over a cuppa, for every word of support, for referring me to clients, for their patience, and for helping me find my Karate Kid moment to choose courage over fear.

In 2020, against the backdrop of a global pandemic, when I was dancing with fear and dodging action because I chose fear to hold me back more than I chose courage to propel me forward, I could not have foreseen the incredible start I have had with my business venture. If I knew then what I know now, I would have ditched fear a long time ago and jumped right in. I would have traded in fear for excitement earlier on in my transition to self-employment. Since leaving my corporate role to become founder of my company, Blackwood Gate Ltd, I've coached business executives, individuals across talent pipelines, partnered with organisations as a coach and facilitator to embed their talent and leadership development programmes, produced my first podcast, been invited to speak on a panel, worked with clients around the world, become an associate board member with the International Coaching Federation UK focused on coaching in organisations, designed coaching-led leadership development solutions, coached leaders to coach their teams for performance, worked 1-2-1 with clients, collaborated with other professional coaches to deliver coach facilitation and team coaching, had my articles published as an associate coach and contributed to this wonderful book, raising funds for Women's Aid inspired by Michelle Gant.

Wow! I look back with huge pride and think, I did that! By

giving yourself permission to take a risk in pursuit of your dreams, it opens up opportunities to meet incredible people and have hugely rewarding experiences. When you realise the power in acknowledging fear, plan for the uncertainty with alternative options, and instead of choosing fear to keep you stuck, choose courage and belief in yourself to move toward being in your element, everything changes. You can achieve anything.

I've reflected greatly on my route to where I am today. A proud founder and director of my own coaching and leadership development company. I'm aware that I actively chose to let fear get in the way of my ambition many times over. Fear of failure, fear of financial lack and loss of security, fear of what others might think if I didn't succeed and the impact of that on my family. Imposter Syndrome was given more space to grow than it deserved and it's voice was loud! Fear was a choice and I was choosing it. I'm not referring to the fear we experience when we feel a true and real threat to our physical safety. What I refer to is the kind of fear we create a false narrative around to help us keep ourselves safe from failure, to stay stuck and keep our dreams and potential out of reach. The fear of vulnerability and the fear that gets us in our own way as our biggest obstacle to change.

What if fear really is a choice? In The Next Karate Kid movie, we hear more wisdom from Mr Miyagi when he says: "Ambition without knowledge is like a boat on dry land". So I leave you with this. Let your ambition be stronger than your fears. Learn about what you fear most and why you fear it. If you are considering a change in your life, become curious about your thoughts and feelings. Your curiosity will raise a level of insight and knowledge that could be a real mindset gamechanger to support your success.

Fear is often manifested through not knowing what's on the other side of a choice. An unsettling sense of uncertainty. Equip yourself with knowledge. Plan for the worst-case scenario you fear the most. Know that, during change, every decision you make is just one decision away from another one. If it doesn't work out, do something different. I have learned that at the point of having an idea about doing something new, taking a different career direction or starting a new venture or relationship, it's too early to choose fear or judge what will be. Instead, gather your resources, have your own back, tap into your network of supporters and plan for the best 'what if' that you can imagine. You've totally got this!

A thing learnt along the way

Say it out loud

The only limitations are the ones we set ourselves.

So don't be afraid to say out loud the goals that you want for yourself. Even if they seem too big, too impossible, too out of reach.

This life is too precious to not go after the things you want.

And the start of that is saying out loud and getting clear on what it is that you want. Without fear or self-judgement.

Life is better when I'm myself

Michelle Gant

There used to be two versions of me.

There was work me: professional, diligent, hardworking, guarded.

And then there was me me: the Michelle who you'd meet down the pub on a Friday or run into at the gym (ok, that's a lie. You would never have run into me at the gym); relaxed, at ease, not overthinking just being.

For a long time I operated under the belief that to get on at work I had to adopt a mask. I would behave how I thought a successful professional would whilst keeping the 'me me' hidden.

Me me. The me who would say how she felt. The me who would express emotion. The me who would share of myself.

I held that me in check, feeling that if I wanted to get on then I had to be someone else – or at least pretend to be. Someone better. Someone cleverer. Someone worthy of having the job title that was somehow showcased on my business card. And it was a feeling that was only strengthened the higher I climbed up the ladder.

Good old imposter syndrome.

But here's what I now know.

That life is much better when we can just be ourselves.

Because when we are ourselves we are more effective, more creative, more able to connect with others. When we are not trying to be who we think we ought to be then we can just relax and bring our whole selves into the party. We can be honest, we can be open, we can be transparent.

When we can just be ourselves, we are set free. Which is fantastic for our wellbeing.

But of course, it isn't always easy to just, well, be.

For me, what happened was that over time I slowly started to let me me into workplace. I would say how I felt, I would tell people about who I was. After a while, a friend and colleague said to me: "It's great when you're just being yourself Michelle." And I realised how right this comment was. I was achieving more, finding new solutions, bringing creativity into what I did. Having fun.

And gradually, I came to a realisation. For a long time, I had been hung up on what people thought of me, or might think of me. For example, I would never, ever talk to people about anything I'd written let alone show them because I was convinced they would either laugh at me or think *who does she think she is?*

But the truth is that they probably weren't thinking anything about me – people have far more to worry about than what I'm getting up to. And if they did, so what? Did it really matter what people thought of me?

Was I going to let it stand in the way of what I wanted to do?

And once I realised that, I decided that I was going to just be, well, me.

It has been incredibly empowering. I have done so many things that I never would have dared to do. Such as this.

Ten years ago, I would never have embarked on a project such as this book. I would never have put a call out for contributors, too scared that people would a) laugh at me b) think who on earth does she think she is, and that I would be humiliated if no-one wanted to take part.

Being my whole self is something that I also want to role model for my daughter too. No doubt she one day will encounter all those feelings that I did along the way. I tell her that I don't let what people think of me or might think of me stop me being, doing, wearing what I want. But she is getting to an age where she does. *"You can wear that hat in the car Mum but not outside,"* she told me. recently. (An animal print beret, I mean, come on!)

It isn't always easy but I know that the world is richer when we are our true selves. And we are happier.

So it's more than ok to just be you.

Fabulous, amazing, wonderful you.

What would you do if you were unconcerned with what others think?

It's clear that one of the barriers that often stops us being ourselves, and pursuing the goals to which we aspire is a concern about what others might think.

Often we are held back by perceptions: our perceptions – mostly erroneous – of how we might be viewed if we are just our whole selves, if we pursue our ambitions.

So, a question that can be useful is this: "what would I do if I was unconcerned with what others think?"

And the answer to this question may reveal a dream that we had hitherto been too afraid to pursue.

References:

66: Aron, Elaine: 'The Highly Sensitive Person' – published 2017

110: Brown, Brené: The Gifts of Imperfection – published 2010

122: Byrne, Rhonda: The Secret – published 2006

148: Karate Kid 3, directed by John G. Avildsen, released 1989

153: The Next Karate Kid, directed by Christopher Cain, released 1994

Your space

This is your space.

Please use it to capture any reflections you have on the things you've read in this book, set out any goals, write down any things you're grateful for, or scribble any thoughts you have that you want to get out on paper.

A BY DAWESY Book!

Mind-Boggling Mini Masterpieces
Ten Tiny Tales
Volume 1

Written and created by

OLIVER DAWES

Illustrated by Snej Mommsen

ISBN 978-1- 9162615-1-8

First published in the UK 2020

www.bydawesy.com

Printed and bound in the UK

THE PIG

Dr Fitzpattenburg was a genius. To most, she was the smartest Earthling ever created, trusted, tried and true. She had engineered a way to save the human race. Time was running out and soon the aliens would come. Their threat to human existence was terrifying. With no option to relocate planets – proving a logistical nightmare – Dr Fitzpattenburg's new shrinking machine meant she could recolonise eight billion Earthlings by injecting them into a single pig. Aliens would have no business with a pig. Oinkington, Snoutsville, Bacon Village and Trotterstown were a few of the suggestions for new areas people could live within The Pig.

Of course, there were protests, alternate proposals, failed scientific solutions and mass hysteria meltdowns … but with the aliens coming and time running out, The Pig was the only option. And so, inside The Pig the humans hid.

Years went by, but the aliens never came. It was a great big stinking lie. Dr Fitzpattenburg made it up! She just didn't like humans and she quite fancied living on planet Earth all by herself. So, once every last being was injected into The Pig, Dr Fitzpattenburg decided not to follow, instead, be alone, a planet of her very own, just her and her pet pig Chopsywopsy.

Sometimes Dr Fitzpattenburg would whisper into Chopsywopsy's ear, "I am God now."

The End

SILENT
SKIN-SHELLS

The sun is shining, I sit outside, I sip my coffee and watch the world go by. But this isn't a world you know. What wanders by isn't warm and fleshy, but cold and floaty. Maybe I should have moved away by now? But I love this coffee shop and I love my home. Not many people stay in the same town for more than a year, it freaks them out, seeing themselves walking by. A ghost from their past. But not me, I quite like it. I find it fascinating watching who I was last year …

What do I mean you must wonder? In my world we shed our skin. Every year when the sun sets on the thirty-first day of the twelfth month – a Silent Skin-Shell leaves our body.

For the rest of time it elegantly and gracefully follows the same path it did that year on a silent rotation over and over. So, if you stayed in the same place for thirty years, you would likely see thirty copies of yourself individually living their lives as you did each year – The ghosts from your past.

Most people can't live in the same home for very long. They would have to live with their ghosts. Millions build their own small hut every year because older homes already contain countless ghosts of other people – walking around, replicating their past lives. The problem is, space is running out, and the Silent Skin-Shells are now everywhere. There are so many the air is almost filled with a fog. A thick fog of ghosts from our pasts. But I like it, I like watching the Silent Skin-Shells and I particularly enjoy spotting my old self.

Sometimes I'll say something like, Oh look, it's me from three years ago, I remember that time, that was the day I went into the green grocers and bought a watermelon. But today I get it wrong; I see myself, but not happily gallivanting with a watermelon. I watch as I cry in the street. That was the day my pet Capybara was sick so I took it to the vets. That was a really sad day. I tried to move on, but now I remember. Maybe it's time for me to depart this town, and leave my ghosts behind.

The End

MR GRUMPY BUTTERCUP

The legend is true. If you hold a buttercup under your chin, the beautiful yellow petals will tell you whether or not you like butter by shining a glorious golden glow, or not, against your skin to confirm your buttery status. In a small village called Churnsville, a miracle graced the flowing pasture. It was the biggest buttercup you ever saw – its stem as strong as a tree stump, its petals brighter than the sun. People came from all over the globe to visit the giant buttery bloom – to show off to their foes a selfie or three with the magnificent flower. But there was one old man who disapproved, a grumpy old soul who lived alone in a single house on top of a hill overlooking the enchanted cup. He tutted and shook his head at the tourists – mumbling profanities as he passed them daily. But one day there was shocking news. The buttercup was gone and the miracle was missing. But it didn't take long to figure it out – the grumpy old man had stolen the prize for himself. But, not in anger, in hope instead – according to the police report here's what they said.

This grumpy old man who hated butter, once had a wife who loved it so. She was called Margarine and their lives were perfect until one day she had to leave him. He found out soon after she couldn't bare to be with a man who despised her passion. The grumpy old man was bitter for years until one day he snapped and stole that cup. He knew it was powerful but what happened was completely unexpected. He assumed such a powerful buttercup would change his hate to love and his darling would return, if only he held its muscular stem and alluring petals under his chin all night long. But instead, as a cheesy full moon graced the skies and the dairy gods spoke, a yellow beam struck his chin and his blood turned to butter. So much so, his body exploded and buttered his walls like an inviting slice of a seeded batch.

The news spread and his wife arrived. The police said, "Don't look," but she burst on in. She wasn't shocked or upset. But, instead, pulled a croissant from her jacket pocket, grabbed a handful of buttery blood and slapped it on her pastry. She then whispered to Mr Grumpy Buttercup, "Oh, I love you now."

The End

LIAM COPPERDALE

Door to door sales was Liam Copperdale's profession. He was magnificent – possibly the best in the country. He was a very handsome man but he worked differently to others. He didn't believe in using his good looks to make a sale, so instead wore a paper bag over his head. Taking a sneak peek out of the window or through the spy hole was enough to put someone off opening the door to Liam Copperdale as they were scared. But, caught unaware and opening the door without pre-warning meant many were stood face to face with a bagged Liam Copperdale and didn't want to close the door in case they seemed rude.

When Liam Copperdale did have the opportunity to sell face to face, or face to bag, bag to face (but never bag to bag) he had a 100% success rate! Why you may wonder? Because Liam Copperdale sold high tech home security systems that meant opening the door to a man with a bag on his head could quickly become a thing of the past.

The End

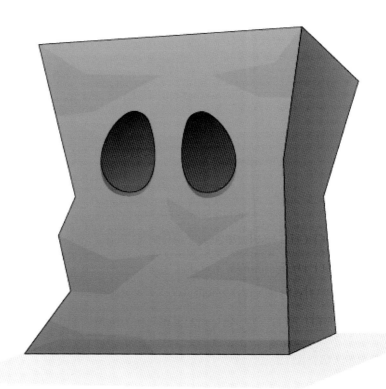

THE FARM SHOP

Mrs Saddlehurst ran a farm shop in the middle of nowhere. No one ever came as the shop smelled of pee. People wondered how she managed to keep things afloat with no custom. But, there was one man that came at the end of every week. Mrs Saddlehurst would keep the shop open Monday-Saturday 09:00-17:00 and on a Sunday 10:00-16:00, yet the man would only ever visit at 15:55 on a Sunday. He would leave with a small jar covered by a brown paper bag. The rest of the week, not a single soul would visit her shop.

Health and safety visited the lonely shop one afternoon and immediately closed it down. The shop only contained jars, hundreds of jars and nothing else. They removed the contents for further testing, concerned at what they'd found. Here's a list:

Goats pee ultra 250mls & 500mls
Goats pee ultra with added saliva 750mls

Pigs pee maximum force 250mls & 500mls
Pigs pee mega mix 150mls

Cows pee supreme 250mls
Cows pee extreme power 500mls

Chickens pee ultimate premium 50mls
Chickens pee superior slushy 20mls

The man had read the local newspaper and was sad to see that health and safety had closed the farm shop down. The following Sunday, as usual, the man visited the shop at 15:55 and read a sign in the window which confirmed the news: 'closed until further notice'. He posted a letter through the door, lightly placed his palm on the door, and then walked away.

Later that evening Mrs Saddlehurst opened the letter and read it out aloud …

Dear Mrs Saddlehurst,

I'm sorry to hear your shop has been shut down, but I'm glad we did business for so long. Although your prices were extortionate – especially the 'Pigs pee mega mix' at an eye watering £8,000 for 150ml, I can assure you, although the health and safety laws are strict in the UK, my sell on fee of £18,000 in Oysterland has been a revelation. Over the course of twenty years whilst we have been doing business, Big-Oyster-Pharma now fully validates that rubbing the ointment into ones face does prevent aging. It's a shame our trading has ended and for now the Oysterlandians will have to age naturally. Let's wait until the dust settles and then maybe talk business again …
In the meantime, I have enclosed a cheque to reimburse any losses until we meet again.

To Mrs Saddlehurst
£2,700,000
Igor Oysterhoft

The End

PHOTO BOOTH

The walls of East Netherington were huge and heavily guarded by robots. Without explanation residents could never leave and outsiders could never enter. It had been this way for hundreds of years. The residents had everything they needed – medical assistance, supermarkets, enter-tainment and homes, but no information or contact with the outside world. On one street stood an old, weathered photo booth. It wasn't plugged in, but every now and then, electrical sparks jumped around it, over it and inside it. Rumours over the years was that if you sat inside the booth it would steal your soul … so from a young age the photo booth was the thing of nightmares.

Every now and then someone would enter

enter that booth – perceived as either insane or too brave for their own good. When you live in a world where you know no different, you tend to 'monkey see, monkey do'. But sometimes you're just born different. Well, that was the view of the government anyway, that's how they decided who would make the cut. Whenever someone did enter the photo booth, as they exited, they were never the same again – they were a shell of their old self.

The government enjoyed the photo booth process. It would steal the mind of whoever sat inside and transfer it to their computer system which would then determine if that person was either crazy or brave. If they were crazy, their mind would be deleted, and if they were brave, their mind would be added to a robot body to live on the outside world as a humanoid. This is why anyone who went into the photo booth came out brain dead. Their minds were stolen!

With a pent up civil war on the horizon due to disputes lasting over one-hundred years between the two remaining colonies on the planet, the government was using East Netherington as a farming plant to produce the bravest humanoids possible to win a war should it break out. The process continues …

The End

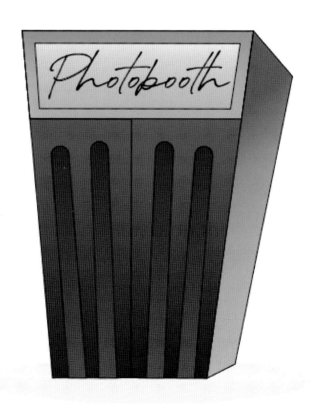

I-SCREAM

The I-Scream van was running low on stock, so a visit to the mortuary was in order to replenish the goods. As soon as Dr Bambagoosga knew the coast was clear and skeleton staff were working – usually around 3am – she would sneak into the mortuary with her large bag and stock up on blood treacle, liver slithers, bone cones and wrinkle sprinkles. She wasn't proud of what she did, but she wanted an early retirement. Being a Doctor paid well, but not as well as the freaks that desired her gruesome treats – those who liked a little extra on their I-Scream.

She would drive her I-Scream van while the stock was fresh and deliver in the dead of night, usually around 4am to a pre-arranged location. So, if your loved one ever mysteriously leaves the house around 4am, and has a hankering for the unusual – maybe, just maybe, they're visiting the I-Scream van for something a little more scary than dairy …

The End

THROUGH
THE GLASS

The year was 2100. People had become lazy, unmotivated, morbidly obese, too tired to move and too stubborn to change.

A fixed benefit to survive was transferred into the accounts of those that didn't want to question the system and were happy to just exist on a quick blast of serotonin delivered via gluttony. The thirst for adventure was no more, but the thirst for sugar was at its peak. Travel was a thing of the past. People were glued to their sofas. They could order any calorie they desired, delivered by drone into their snack hatch like a privileged rabbit hutch. They stare into their screens with an unlimited amount of sugar-coated, brainwashing TV – so much had been produced over the past two-hundred years that there was enough on screen entertainment to keep you glued for one hundred lazy lifetimes. They were set for life. Eat, watch, sleep, repeat. No need to leave the house. For the few in control, big business was in window TVs. You could buy a window package which meant you lived anywhere in the world from the comfort of your own chair. Take a look outside … Monday: mountains with wonderful waterfalls. Tuesday: tsunamis that couldn't destroy your home, a thrill to be had! Or perhaps a weekend away … Saturday and Sunday: sunny beaches, wicked waves and beautiful blue skies. No need to leave your house.

The glass is cold to the touch, but warm to the soul and hot to those in control. No need to leave your house. No need to buy a door. Spend it on a window TV instead and lose yourself through the glass.

The End

CRUMBS

Sweep, sweep, sweep, scoop, scoop, scoop, pour, pour, pour and sleep, sleep, sleep. This was the daily routine of Agathoramax, a huge but gentle monster that lived on Earth.

Agathoramax didn't like the other monsters, they were mean and relentless. They would eat whatever and whoever stood in their way – swipe, crunch, swallow and repeat. But the crumbs, oh the crumbs! Agathoramax would despair. What a mess those awful monsters would leave – on every surface, remains of their meals left to rot.

Agathoramax was a beautiful soul, she did not take pleasure in eating the same foods as the other monsters, and certainly did not like cleaning up after them. But how was Agathoramax supposed to enjoy living on Earth unless the human crumbs were swept up. Remove the reminder, remove the smell, one day it may stop and she can wave farewell! The other monsters certainly wouldn't do it. So left to Agathoramax it was.

If she stopped, she would become overwhelmed, if she kept going, she could hope it would end.

So she would grab her broom, frown upon those human crumbs – sweep, sweep, sweep, scoop, scoop, scoop, pour, pour, pour then sleep, sleep, sleep.

The End

STONES

Whenever Griffin Rhodes got out his pouch of coins to pay for something, people would point and laugh. Not because he had a pouch, but because when he poured his coins into his hand, four precious stones would nestle neatly in his palm. People would ask, "Why? What's a man to do with random stones?" Griffin would gently reply, "I quite like them, they make me feel good. Besides, I've had this feeling for a while, a deep fulfilling feeling I'm supposed to carry these stones." But, people would shrug and repeat that same old question, "What's a man to do with random stones?"

One dark winter's morning, Griffin Rhodes awoke from a very deep sleep. He opened the curtains and squinted his eyes.

Something was unusual, something was different. He placed his hand on the window and felt heat, a heat unknown to a winter's morn. Then a flash of lightning, but none like he'd ever seen. The colour was curious, it was neon green. As quick as a flash, to find out more, he put on his trousers and was about to exit the door. One last stretch, his arms reached up high, when all of a sudden the roof ripped into the sky. A demon swooped in and grabbed Griffin Rhodes by his out-stretched arms. He screamed so loud but felt it was too late.

As the demon held him in its hand, Griffin could see right across the land. There were other demons with humans in their hands, all begging for their lives, trying to pay their way out. Griffin pleaded, "Where am I, what do you want?" The demon replied, "You're on the other side and eat you I will."
"But wait, I can pay, I can give you whatev-er you want." The demon laughed and